This is the first book I have ever written and there are a few people that I would like to say Thank You to before getting started:

Thank you to my incredible, intelligent and beautiful wife - Mrs. Anonymous. You have given me a great gift by allowing me to take the time necessary to write this book. I will always love you.

Thank you to the rest of my family and friends for listening to my crypto talks.

Thank you to my kids for not thinking less of me when you are old enough to be reading these pages. I love each of you with all my heart.

Thank you to Cori for teaching me how to edit a book. The work you did helped me tremendously.

PROLOGUE

This book was written over the course of two years between 2021-2023.

The person who invented Bitcoin is unknown to the world. Until now. In the pages to follow, I will reveal the true identity of Satoshi Nakamoto.

The names of the people in this book have been hidden in order to protect the innocent.

This book is non-fiction written with some fiction sprinkled in to make it more interesting for the reader.

If you want to learn about cryptocurrency, I hope that I am able to educate you, or at least spur enough interest in your mind to inspire you to seek further knowledge from somebody who has even more experience than me. I do not know everything about crypto. Not by a longshot. But I do know more than most people.

I am here to warn you all of an impending disaster. You can choose to believe it or not.

THE CRYPTO BOOK THAT YOU NEED TO READ

Written by: Mr Anonymous

Chapter 1: INTRODUCTION TO BITCOIN

I always knew I'd be rich. Or at least I always thought it. When I was a young kid I figured success would come from playing in the NBA for the Boston Celtics. When I was in high school and college I thought it would be on Wall St as a stock broker. It didn't happen though. Real life looked more like this: I was a New Hampshire guy who went to a NH college and stayed local after graduating. Met a girl a year later and got married. And divorced. Then got married and divorced again to someone different. Which just about catches you up to where I am now. Married again….but not divorced. Happily married this time. But not rich. Not yet. It's coming though. And I have decided to write to tell you all about how.

Bitcoin.

You have probably heard the word by now I'm guessing. I would also guess that you have absolutely no clue what it really is. How it works. What it does. What it is being used for and what it will be used for. You probably also have no clue whatsoever about the many other cryptocurrencies that are out there. Bitcoin has been around for over 10 years yet most people are clueless about it. Plenty of other cryptos are being created every month, and most people are also clueless about them. But the people who do know about them have been getting rich. I am in the process of becoming one of those people.

"Honey, can we talk about something else?"

She's right. It is her birthday after all. We are all dressed up and out at an incredible restaurant. She looks like a million bucks. She is always beautiful, but when she does her hair and makeup my wife truly becomes next level gorgeous. Movie star caliber beautiful. And tonight she has on a skirt that shows just enough leg and high heels. I've always been a sucker for high heels. They just make a woman's legs and ass look so ripe. But I digress…

"You are right." And she is right. I talk about crypto all the fucking time. I can't stop thinking about it. I tell her stories about how "this coin is pumping" or how "this mining pool dumped a bunch of coins" etc, etc. She doesn't care about most of it. But she likes to see me so passionate. And she likes when I tell her how rich we are going to be when things go parabolic. But she doesn't need to hear any of this right now. It's her birthday. Tonight needs to be about her.

"What else should we talk about?" I ask, secretly hoping that she might come up with something that involves her taking off the skirt while leaving on the high heels. At this point I drift off in thought and can't remember what she responds with…

Cryptocurrency has been my whole life for the past couple of years. Sure, I have spent time helping to raise our two young children (I have a third child who lives with her mother). But outside of the time with the kids, crypto has been the center of my universe; a position that is more than justifiable. My incredibly hot wife and I currently have over 500k in crypto. In December of 2020, one Bitcoin was worth $20,000 US dollars. Now here we are in March of 2021 and one bitcoin is worth 51k. Let me do the math for you: That's a 150% increase in three months! Bitcoin isn't the only crypto we own, but it is the most well-known. There are a handful of other coins in our portfolio, and those have been going up like crazy too. But we have invested the most money in Bitcoin, and there is good reason why. Bitcoin is what got me into the crypto game in the first place. And it is at the center of the global crypto market.

I was first introduced to Bitcoin back in 2013 during a night of bar hopping with my future (and current) wife. A friend of her's had asked me if I knew what bitcoin is, since I had been working in technology since 1999.

"Nope. What is it?" I answered.

He did his best to explain, but either his effort was lacking or my interest was extraordinarily difficult to capture at that moment due to a solidly achieved level of intoxication. What I do remember is that he described it as being some kind of internet money that cost $300 apiece. No way I was interested in something like that. What a dumbass.

Fast forward to the year 2017. I stumbled across bitcoin again somehow. Not sure how or why, but this time something clicked differently than it did back in 2013. This time, I was intrigued and wanted to learn more. So I bought a book that would change my life forever.

SIDE NOTE: I DO NOT REMEMBER THE NAME OF THE BOOK THAT I AM REFERENCING HERE. I LOANED IT OUT TO SOMEONE ONCE AND THEY NEVER RETURNED IT.

This book started out by explaining the origin of money. It explained how the barter system was first developed as an agreement through which one party agreed to give something in exchange for something from another party. Then at some point the barter system needed improvement because of a desire to better measure the value of items. Two people wishing to exchange goods sometimes found it difficult to make the exchange because one good was substantially more valuable than the other.

According to the book, the first society to create a system to measure the value of goods did so by using a rare type of rock that was only found in their area. They essentially formed a first "bank", through which people would take out loans and hold these rare rocks as collateral. I'm not going to go into details beyond this for a few reasons:

One – I don't 100% remember the details of the story so I'm not really sure about how the whole system worked.

Two – It isn't that relevant to what we are discussing here.

Three- I'm lazy. You will see this clearly demonstrated if you continue reading.

The book went on to explain that money only has value because of the perceived value that society gives it. A dollar bill is essentially a useless piece of paper. But because the government has printed a number on it and assigned a value to it - be it 5,10,20, 100 – we as citizens agree it has that level of value. Until we don't. And until it doesn't. Those rocks are the same as the paper that money is printed on. You can't eat them when times get tough and ultimately neither rock nor paper has much utility on its own. This concept is what I was able to grasp as the primary reason why Bitcoin has the potential to increase in value. Scarcity. If people can agree that Bitcoin has value, the limited supply aspect of the digital coin will drive demand. Simple economics.

To take things a bit further, governments all around the world spend more money than they take in, and The United States is the biggest offender. This cannot go on forever. I will say it again.

This. Cannot. Go. On. Forever.

The United Stated has a national debt of over $30 trillion. The deficit for 2021 alone was over $2.75 trillion. In my mind, this absolutely demands a step back for evaluation. We owe $30 trillion. And in 2021 we borrowed another $2.75 trillion. Forget about paying the $30 trillion back. We need to first think about getting back to just breaking even for one year! That $30 trillion in debt that we have is never going to be paid back and we must find a solution to the debt problem as soon as possible. How can people not realize this? The insanity of it all drives me crazy.

Speaking of driving me crazy - my wife is ready to leave the restaurant. Our dinner was awesome. Perfectly cooked steaks. A nice bottle of red wine. Some crazy good chocolate lava cake for dessert. And now it is time to leave to go find something to do. Something that doesn't involve food or crypto or national debts. Hopefully it involves taking off those shoes and that skirt. Yep. It's time to go. I'm gonna pay the bill and get outta here.

Chapter 2: WHY BITCOIN, SATOSHI?

"In order to capture a city, first capture the heart of the people."

That is the fortune that I got last night inside of my Chinese cookie. I am a big fan of the "all things happen for a reason" way of thinking, so this little white piece of paper inside of that yummy crunchy cookie got my wheels a spinnin'. If I'm going to get you people to want to learn about bitcoin, I'm going to need to first get you to like me. But how do I go about doing that?

I have no experience with writing a book. I have limited knowledge of how to create a "hook" to get you people interested. My ability to do proper "character development" is probably lacking. I am sure I use the word "I" too much in my writing and I'm 100% positive that I use "air quotes" entirely too often. But I am going to try my best to just be myself and hope that is enough for you. Please though – Have patience.

My neck is not in great shape. Random comment, I know. But it is top of mind right now and has been for the past few days. Actually, it has been close to top of mind for almost 30 years now. Ever since that girl driving her car on the other side of the road crossed over the yellow line and rammed straight into me. Head on. I estimate we were both going around 30 miles an hour when impact happened. It was snowing and our brakes didn't allow us much opportunity to slow down. My head went right into the windshield of my little Nissan Sentra because I was stupidly not wearing a seat belt. Ended up chipping a tooth and cutting open my knee from it slamming into the fuze box during impact. Had some other minor injuries too but it was my neck that got really messed up. In the ambulance on the way to the hospital I can remember asking the EMT "Am I going to die?" Turns out, I was being melodramatic. I was going to be just fine.

Except for my neck. I have seen doctors and chiropractors for more than 25 years now. In 2020, I herniated a disk in my neck and underwent surgery to have two vertebrae fuzed together. C6 and C7 for those of you in the know. Seems like it's a somewhat common injury/remedy for people who spend a lot of time staring at computers. But wow was it a painful ordeal for me! I now always worry about *having that herniated disk problem flare up again. Working at the computer aggravates my injury.*

I tell you this because as I stand here typing right now, my neck is sending a neon light flashing message to my brain alerting me to change my posture. The pressure is building up in my shoulders and lower neck. But I have been typing like this for almost 30 years. I don't know any other way.

But enough about me. Let's get back to what you really came to hear about.

Before I fully dive into the rantings of a cryptocurrency addicted madman, let's make sure that all of you readers have a basic foundation of Bitcoin knowledge. Wikipedia says: "On January 3rd, 2009, the Bitcoin network came into existence with Satoshi Nakamoto mining the genesis block of bitcoin, which had a reward of 50 Bitcoins. Embedded in the coinbase of this block was the text: The Times Jan/03/2009 Chancellor on brink of second bailout for banks."

INFO: "Embedded in the coinbase of this block" means that there was a message added to the blockchain of the Bitcoin network.

The Bitcoin network started running on Jan 3, 2009. That part of the text is easy enough to understand. Let's break down what the rest of the text refers to. It was on October 31, 2008, that Satoshi Nakamoto, the developer of Bitcoin, published the bitcoin whitepaper. Weeks earlier, on September 15, 2008, Lehman Brothers had filed for bankruptcy in the United States. This was the largest bankruptcy case in United States history and it essentially kicked off a financial crisis that spread to the rest of the world. Lehman was the fourth largest investment bank in the US at the time and had been in operation since its founding in 1850! Then one day, kaput. Bad loans, mortgage defaults, and a variety of other financial product failures combined to spread contagion throughout the farthest of far corners of the entire planet.

Then, just 45 days after Lehman declared bankruptcy, came the introduction of Bitcoin. This timing was not a coincidence. The "Chancellor on brink of second bailout for banks" line written into the code of the genesis block tells us that the creator of Bitcoin was none too happy about the state of the worldwide financial

system - a system that is largely quarterbacked by the United States of America.
INFO: The genesis block is the first blockchain recording on the Bitcoin network.

So who is it that created the Bitcoin network? Who is it that typed those words into the initial block for all of history to see? That's the coolest part of the whole bitcoin story, in my opinion. And it is the #1 reason why I decided to write this book. Nobody knows who invented bitcoin. We do have a name - Satoshi Nakamoto. But that name is a pseudonym. Satoshi is just a meme - a fictional character, who for all intents and purposes, invented blockchain technology, thereby proving himself or herself as one of the most gifted minds in the history of the world.

For those of you that don't know, blockchain technology is essentially a decentralized application – a software app that runs on a bunch of computers at one time without any of the computers being "in charge". They are all equal. This arrangement makes a blockchain incredibly difficult to hack because there is no central "location" to target. This is an extremely simplified overview, but for now please take my word for it that blockchain technology is absolutely next level futuristic type stuff. And Satoshi introduced the world to it. In my opinion, it stands to reason that a person (or group of people) who is so incredibly intelligent, must have a reason for wanting to remain anonymous. Someone that smart has a plan. And that plan is playing out. Day by day. Month by month. Year by year.

SIDE NOTE: I AM GOING TO INTERJECT WITH SIDE NOTES WHENEVER I FEEL LIKE YOU, THE READER, MIGHT NEED A BREAK. THERE IS A TON OF INFO IN THIS BOOK, AND IT WILL BE HARD TO RETAIN SOME OF IT. IF YOU EVER FEEL LOST IN THE WORDS, JUST PLEASE GO AHEAD AND SKIP TO THE START OF THE NEXT CHAPTER.

When the Bitcoin network first started running, Satoshi and a couple other people were the only folks running the software. Satoshi invited a couple of other developers to work on the project with him anonymously, and they would bounce the software back and forth between themselves, making updates as they went. Eventually they started processing "transactions" by which they would send each other bitcoin. **INFO: You don't have to buy or sell or send an entire Bitcoin. You can use fractional pieces of Bitcoin.** As Satoshi and his developing network of users sent transactions back and forth to one another, the software would monitor the recording of these transactions on the blockchain to make sure that everything was recording correctly. If something didn't work correctly as they scaled, they would develop new software code and add it into the program. Fix the bug, rework it, and then upgrade and move forward with all of the computers now working with the upgraded version of the software.

This is how the Bitcoin network works: A computer runs software that essentially competes to solve a string of math problems as quickly as possible. Once one of the computers solves the last math problem in a string, it sends out a message to the other computers. Then these other computers verify that the problem solved by the winning computer is correct, and they record that information in something called a digital ledger. This is called a Proof of Work (POW) system of verification. Basically, what happens is that the computers make a stamp in the application for all users – past, present, and future - to see as proof that a transaction occurred. After a certain number of problems are solved by the computers, the software creates a reward for the computer that solved the last problem in the string or "block". In this way, the computers, ie miners, are all competing against each other to win a race to solve the math problems, and thereby get rewarded. The "rewards" are Bitcoin, which get sent to the Bitcoin address (wallet) that is associated with the winning miner. One solved block for Bitcoin in the year 2022 is worth a reward of 6.25 BTC. **INFO: BTC is the coin name that is used for Bitcoin.** When the Bitcoin network originally started, the reward for one block was 50 Bitcoin. The process of rewards decreasing in half from 50 down to 25 to 12.5 to 6.25 through the years is a result of something called the halvening or halving. These halvenings occur approximately once every four years.

SIDE NOTE: I TOLD YOU THIS COULD GET COMPLICATED WITH INFO. BUT THIS NEXT PARAGRAPH IS ONE OF THE MOST IMPORTANT IN THE ENTIRE BOOK. PAY ATTENTION.

One of the most important characteristics of Bitcoin is that there is a preset total supply of BTC that will ever be mined. 21 million. That is why the halvenings are so important. The final Bitcoin (by then it will be fractional pieces of Bitcoin) is projected to be mined in the year 2140. As of 2022, approximately 19 million have already been mined. I will explain more about this later in our chapter about miners.

Let's get back to the discussion of Satoshi. One of the smartest people to ever walk the earth creates a completely new type of technology that grows to a level where it becomes universally recognized as having value – and then to the point where a country actually recognizes it as a form of national currency. **INFO: El Salvador acknowledged Bitcoin as a national currency in 2021.** And that person wants to remain anonymous? Someone smart enough to create new Internet money, that has grown to a level where one of these coins as of today in September of 2023 is worth more than $26,000, doesn't want anyone to know who they are. Think about that. Think about why that person might want to keep his or her identity hidden from the rest of the world. Seems kinda sketchy.

Want even more sketchy? Satoshi actually still owns more than 1 million Bitcoin. It is difficult to determine exactly how many, but you can tell from the dates when the Bitcoin were received that they all belong to the same wallets as the ones that were initially created by Satoshi, mined during the initial days and months of BTC and just left to grow old and dusty. 1 million Bitcoin. Multiply that by the price of BTC today would you please? The answer tells us that today Satoshi owns tens of billions worth of US dollars in Bitcoin that has never been touched. Why hasn't he sold any of it? Makes you wonder, doesn't it? But I digress…..

As I have jokingly said through the years, there are two groups of people who own Bitcoin. One is software developers. These are the smartest people you knew back in high school. The other group of people that own Bitcoin are the extremely rich individuals who have extra money to make speculative investments in fake Internet money. So I ask you, whose side would you rather be on?

    A. The really smart people and really rich people
    B. Everybody else

The answer is pretty obvious to me. You should want to be on the side of an individual who is so smart that he can create this technology, do so anonymously, and have it rise to a level where nations are acquiring it as a replacement for their national currency. Why is Bitcoin so appealing?

Consider this: When you go to the store and use your credit card to buy something, there are actually approximately seven different vendors involved with that transaction. This is why transactions sometimes take days to be fully processed on your statements of activity. The vendor where you are buying something needs to use the PoS (Point of Sale – not Piece of Shit) terminal to communicate with the credit card company who connects with their bank to approve the transaction. Then the money gets sent from that bank to the bank of the vendor where you are making the purchase. In the existing traditional payments system, there are companies at each of the stops making a bit of revenue on the transaction. With blockchain technology - distributed ledger technology - those transactions get recorded and settled within a matter of minutes. And some cryptos can actually process transactions in seconds or split seconds. The coins simply go from one wallet to another. Transaction completed.

Cryptocurrency is the next step in the evolution of money. It is superior technology, plain and simple.

Chapter 3: GAMBLING AND MINERS

At this time, it might be appropriate to let the reading community know that I have lost over half a million dollars during my lifetime of gambling. Way over 500k. At some point I STOPPED counting, but it's definitely over 500k. I'm 49 years old and I started gambling when I was around 13. It began with pitching quarters against sidewalks with my friends. As we got older, we moved to playing games of pig in basketball for packs of baseball cards. Then one day we took bike rides down to a neighborhood gas station and I got up the courage to buy a scratch ticket. I was only around 14 years old at the time and you were supposed to be 18 years old to buy them, but apparently the store clerks didn't care much about adhering to those guidelines back then. I was sold the ticket, and I remember hitting for 40 bucks. Man, I was the hero of the group that day. "Let's go to the baseball card store and spend it!" And that's what we did. I bought everyone some cards. It was fun to be the hero.

Eventually I started going to the racetracks to bet on the horses and dogs. Once I got a car, my friends and I would skip school every now and then just to go to the track. I'd lose way more often than I ever won, but when I won it felt so good. I liked beating the system. The fact that the system was slowly but surely taking all my money didn't seem to register, so my gambling problem kept growing. In February of 1997, the New England Patriots were playing the Green Bay Packers in the Super Bowl and that seemed like the ideal time to pay a visit for the first time to Sin City. Las Vegas. The Patriots were going to beat the Brett Favre led Green Bay Packers easily. I was sure of it. So sure, that I asked my younger sister to borrow a large chunk of her life savings, $3,000, if memory serves me correctly. I would pay her back extra once they won, I promised. I brought along about $7,000 of my own money too. (Most of it was from cash advances on credit cards). And I laid it in.

The Patriots ended up losing that Super Bowl by 14 points. The spread on the game was 14 points, so I broke even on a chunk of my bets, but a multi thousand dollar chunk of the bet was on the moneyline for the game. That means the Pats had to win the game outright. So I lost those thousands. And then, of course, I lost the thousands I had gotten back on the +14 bet push. Alcohol and blackjack and whatever other table games I chose to play all worked together as a team to take my cash. And my sister's cash. (I'm pretty sure I paid her all of that money back eventually). And if memory serves me correctly, I promised myself that I would stop gambling forever after that weekend. Yeah.

The years go by and I proceed to lose thousands and thousands every year to bookies betting on football, basketball, baseball, etc. I go to Vegas approximately 30 times over the next 20 years, never coming out on the positive side of things during even a single trip. I lose money on pyramid schemes, horse racing, casinos, fantasy sports leagues, and even on simple straight up wagers with friends. I'm an easy target. I'm the MUSH. That's what my circle of friends calls me because they know it's true. MUSH. I single handedly can make a winning bet turn into a losing one. And through time I have come to accept my fate as an absolutely atrocious gambler. But what I have also come to find out is that all of those gambling losses were simply preparation for the insanity that comes with putting your life savings into the cryptocurrency market.

The day to day and week to week price swings in crypto can absolutely drive most people out of their minds. It is not uncommon to have price swings of 10-20% or even more within a 24 hour period. And when these price swings happen, you have opinions coming in from all angles. If you follow the crypto communities on social media, your brain will be bombarded with reasons to buy, hold, sell, go all in, get out, leverage trade, speculate, etc. I find myself amused at how one minute I feel like I should sell a large position and then literally minutes later I feel like I should be buying. During these times I feel the exact same type of adrenaline-fueled rush that I get from gambling.

Back in the middle of 2017 after I had done a reasonably extensive amount of research on the crypto market, I decided that we should move into the space with aggression. Let's gamble! We had approximately 30k in savings that we could quickly get our hands on, so we bought a little BTC to start with and then we bought some ETH. **INFO: ETH is the coin name for ethereum.** These were the two coins I knew the most about. With bitcoin, I loved that it was the name recognized leader in the crypto space. ETH I loved for different reasons. Yes, it was the #2 largest coin and it had a large following of people on social media who believed it would be going up. But the part that intrigued me most is the fact that ethereum is built with a different type of technological framework that can allow for various applications (ie coins) to run on top of it.

INFO: Bitcoin was created with the ability for me to send you BTC, and vice versa. We can send BTC back and forth for various reasons. We can use it to buy stuff. Or we can hold it. Ethereum was built with a next level technology - the ability for you and me to execute something called smart contracts. What's a smart contract? Think of it this way: Ethereum is a highway. A road is built, paved, etc and now we can use the road to get to various destinations. What do we want to do when we get to the various destinations? That's up to each of us. The road just helps us get there and provides an agreed upon pathway to follow. Ethereum is the highway. Most of the other coins (ie altcoins) you hear about are cars that run along that highway. Many of these smaller market cap coins are simply software applications built on the Ethereum network with the purpose of accomplishing a specific task. These altcoins don't run on the bitcoin network because they can't. Only Bitcoin runs on the Bitcoin network. That's a big difference between ETH and BTC.

The purpose of the ETH coin is to power the transactions that take place on the ethereum network, whether it is ETH being sent or an altcoin that operates on or integrates with the ethereum network. A smart contract is an agreement for a transaction to be executed once an action has occurred. Once an agreed upon action has been completed, the network is alerted, thereby triggering an outcome. This outcome is typically a release of funds – whereby ETH, or the relevant altcoin, is sent to the appropriate party.

When it came time to actually invest a large chunk of our 30k, I wasn't sure of the best way to do it. I spent a few thousand dollars buying BTC and ETH, but then I needed to decide if we should go ahead and buy 2 whole BTC for $26,000 (the cost of one bitcoin at the time in 2017 was $13,000) and use just about all of our money…..or should we sprinkle it around into other cryptos too? There were tons of new coins hitting the market and many of them seemed to have an interesting pitch. Plus, all of them seemed to be going up, and most of them were going up at a much more accelerated rate percentagewise than Bitcoin. I wanted to invest our money, but what would be the best way?

As I spent more time researching on the Internet, I began to learn about how miners are used to power the Bitcoin network. This was an incredible revelation to me at the time. I discovered that miners would get paid in Bitcoin for dedicating their processing power to the network. From what I could tell, there was an 800 pound gorilla in the mining space called Bitmain that made the very best miners. Their main product was something called an Antminer. **INFO: Antminers are specialized computers that power the bitcoin network. That is their sole purpose – to solve the math problems.** And they were expensive and tough to get ahold of. Bitmain was based in China, and to buy a brand new one directly from China you needed to wait weeks or even months for it to be delivered. Plus, you needed to pay for the Antminers in a crypto called Bitcoin Cash. Bitcoin Cash came about as the result of a fork in the Bitcoin network, a subject that we will address later on. **INFO: BCH is the symbol ticker for Bitcoin Cash. Even though it is called Bitcoin Cash and has the word Bitcoin in the name, BCH is an entirely different coin than BTC.** I wasn't sure why you needed to pay in BCH and the whole process just seemed more difficult than it needed to be. So instead of buying a new one, we just went on Amazon and bought a used Antminer from there. Nice and easy. $4,000 and it arrived within a few days. Instead of buying cryptos with our 30k, we would invest in miners and hopefully spend less money to acquire the same amount of bitcoin through time!

INFO: BTC is mined via a Proof of Work (PoW) method. This means that the computers do the work of solving the math problems and then publish the results for all other computers to see. Most other cryptocurrencies are mined via a Proof of Stake (PoS) method in which a group of large coin holders validate the transactions by committing their coins to the network. These groups of coin holders essentially give their "aok" approval to transactions as they hit the network. There is plenty of info out on the Web for you to read if you want to dive deeper into this, but the main reason for people endorsing PoS versus PoW is that PoS systems use much less energy to power the network.

While we were researching the best way to go about getting our hands on an Antminer, we also were exploring what pieces we needed to build an Ethereum focused mining system that most people called a "rig". The Ethereum rig was much more complex to set up than the Antminer. With the rig, we needed to buy a handful of ultra powerful GPU cards. The cards from nvidia seemed to be the best, so naturally they were the most expensive. They were also in very low supply. I didn't know it at the time, but tons of people were getting into the mining game back then because there was so much money to be made. Yes, the upfront cost could be substantial, but once the rig was built and ready to roll, depending on what coins you were mining you could potentially make all of your money back in just a matter of months. The nvidia cards we bought cost in the range of $400 apiece (we bought 6 of them) and the rest of the rig system including the connection pieces and CPU cost somewhere in the 3k range.

SIDE NOTE: YOU HAVE ALMOST MADE IT TO THE END OF THIS CHAPTER. YOU CAN DO IT!

Once an Antminer or any mining rig is set up, the only cost the owner incurs is the electricity needed to power the machine. Depending on the size of the rig though, the power cost can be extensive. For example: The monthly added cost to our electric bill after running the Antminer at home was roughly $200 a month. The Antminer was way way way too loud to keep at the office where I worked, so we had to keep it at home in the basement. With the mining rig that we set up for ETH, we let that run at the office. It was much quieter. My estimate was that the power usage was probably in the same ballpark as the Antminer, but because I didn't pay for power at the office, I never saw a bill. That made the ETH mining rig essentially free to run.

Long story short - After a few months, the whole mining operation turned into a pain in the ass. I am not a technical individual by nature. My wife is. But it became a bother for me to have to ask her to fix little technical issues that seemed to pop up more consistently than I would have liked. Plus by the end of 2017 the price of bitcoin started to go down and so did the amount of coin rewards that we were receiving from our miners. I ended up packing up the pieces and selling both the Antminer and the components of the mining rig on eBay. I think I got about $1200 for the Antmimer and in total I got about 2k for the mining rig and GPU cards. In all, we took a loss at the time, but as time has played out and the price of BTC has risen again, the BTC and other coins that we mined have all gone up to a level where we have actually made money on the mining rig experiment. All we needed to do was hodl. **INFO: The term hodl is used in crypto to signify holding onto a coin for the long term.** And the knowledge gained throughout the entire process was incredibly helpful. Let me share more of that knowledge with you. But I will do so in a new chapter. This one is getting a little lengthy. And to be honest, I doubt the ability for some of you to maintain focus during the educational pieces of this book. Truth be told, I would probably be falling asleep right about now.

CHAPTER 4: LEARN FROM MY MISTAKES!

Considerate.

If I had to use one word to describe myself, considerate would be it. I care how others feel. I want them to be happy. But being considerate in this world can be a difficult cross to carry. So many people are just flat out mean or too stupid to even deserve any help. As a naturally considerate person, you want to try to help everyone, but then you sometimes get angry and frustrated because you question whether people deserve your help.

During my life, I have made three full length movies in which I was the creator, director and lead actor. Each of the movies is over ninety minutes long. Each of the movies was created with the intention of trying to make the world a better place.

My first movie, Power To The People, was filmed in New York City a couple of months after 9/11. That attack on our country left me gutted and crushed. So much pain caused to so many people. I felt like I had to try to do something to help. So I went to New York City and walked the streets trying to interview people who might be appealing characters for my movie. That's when I bumped into a black dude named Casey on the subway. He was about 6' 3" tall and in good shape with a nice smile. We talked for a minute and then I asked him a question.

"Hey Casey. I'm in NYC making a movie trying to help people. You have any interest in being in the movie?"

This guy was a total stranger. But years ago you could actually interact with someone on a NYC subway without taking your life into your hands.

"A movie?" he questioned. I noticed the confused and skeptical look on his face.

"Yeah", I answered him. "It will only take a couple of minutes. I just want to interview you real quick and get it on video."

We talked for another minute or so, and then he agreed to be in the movie.

"OK", I said. "Here we go." I took out my camcorder and hit the record button.

"Hello Everyone. This is Casey. I just met him on the subway here in New York City and he agreed to let me interview him for Power To The People. Casey. If you had ONE thing you could say to the world, what would it be?"

Keep in mind that this was January of 2002. There were no cell phones back then. There was no TikTok. No Facebook. No Twitter (X). None of it. We were in the beginning days of reality TV, and these were the earliest days of people trying to go "viral". I wanted Casey to help get me there. **INFO: The very first reality TV show ever was The Real World. It first aired on MTV back in 1993.**

"What would I tell the world?" he repeated back to me. "That's a tough question. I just met this guy here on the subway. I don't even know his name. What's your name? (I replied with my name). Well, I met (him) on the subway. We started talking and now I'm here on camera.

What would I say to the world?" he said out loud again. He sighed and exhaled. "If you do everything with love in your heart, things will turn out ok. Everyone may not like you or agree with you, but if you do everything with love in your heart people aren't going to dislike you. And what you give out to the world comes back to you. You receive what you put out into the world."

We exchanged a few additional comments from there. Then I said thanks to Casey and stopped the camera. We shook hands and then I gave him 50 bucks. The look on his face was one of happy surprise.

Maybe Casey went on to sell millions of copies of self-help books. Or maybe he went on to be just a regular nobody like me. I have no clue. I knew him for only five minutes of my life. But he was in my first movie. And now he is in my first book.

"What you give out to the world comes back to you."

That message stands the test of time. And whether or not I am successful, I am always going to try to help people.

When the Bitcoin network first started running, Satoshi and his circle of miners simply used their home or work computers to mine coins. They didn't need extra powerful machines because there wasn't a lot of competition; there were not a lot of computers on the network. But as word spread about this new technology called Bitcoin, the techies of the world wanted to try it out. They downloaded the software and played with things to see how it all worked. They created Bitcoin wallets for themselves and directed the computers to send their BTC rewards directly to the wallets when their machine solved a block. As time passed, many of the people forgot about their wallets, and as a result, a chunk of these early Bitcoin experimenters didn't end up profiting from it. This is an absolutely crazy part of the history of Bitcoin!

Many of the home computers that the techies used to mine Bitcoin were disposed of through time as normal people might do periodically with their computers as they upgrade for new ones. A large number of these owners forgot all about the Bitcoin wallets they had created and plenty of these people probably have no clue whatsoever how much BTC they even had. Keep in mind, for the first few years of Bitcoin's existence, BTC was essentially worthless. Nobody was using it for anything. **INFO: The first documented example of a person buying something using Bitcoin was on May 22, 2010.** A programmer in Florida named Laszlo Hanyecz paid someone 10,000 BTC to have 2 Papa John's pizzas delivered to his house. No businesses accepted Bitcoin at the time, but the person who had the pizzas delivered to Laszlo paid for them himself in exchange for the 10,000 BTC. There were very limited ways to acquire it. There was almost no resale market. And only the hardcore geeks even knew it existed. If you were one of these hardcore geeks who managed to mine a bunch of Bitcoin, even if you had hundreds or thousands of them in your wallet, there was nothing you really could do with them. It was just a cool experiment you were a part of. **INFO: It is estimated that millions of Bitcoins are lost forever because people got rid of their computers and are unable to find their private keys. Private keys are a series of letters/numbers used to encrypt data to secure a crypto wallet.**

As time went on, more and more techies downloaded the Bitcoin software. That meant there was now more competition amongst the computers to try to be the winning machine that solved a block. This spurred a movement to acquire more and more powerful computers, ultimately leading to the creation of Bitcoin dedicated computers and the founding of China based company Bitmain in 2013. There will be more on this later in the book.

Mining on the Ethereum network similarly grew through time (**INFO: The Ethereum network started in 2013**) and resulted in the desire for more and more powerful machines. The faster a rig can compute equations, the more likely that machine will solve the last equation of the block and thereby receive rewards. When setting up our Ethereum based rig we had a variety of GPU cards that we could install, but as I mentioned earlier, the nvidia cards worked the fastest, so we bought those.

What I eventually discovered was that even if our machine, be it the Antminer or the ETH focused mining rig, was not the machine that solved the last equation of a block, we could still be able to get rewards. To accomplish this, we joined something called a mining pool. **INFO: Mining pools are communities of miners that join together to give the group a better chance of solving a block. Power in numbers.** Think about it: If you have one lonely machine competing against thousands and thousands of other machines, it is possible, in fact quite probable, that you could run your machine all the time and actually never receive any rewards because your computer wasn't the one to finish a block. As the price of Bitcoin increased through time and more people got into mining, people realized that if there was a way to join together, their chances of receiving some rewards would be greater. Then they could simply split the rewards amongst themselves. Some is better than none. Eventually large mining farms were formed in an effort to be able to guarantee someone returns. **INFO: For years Bitmain has owned a couple of the largest mining pools in the world - BTC.com and Antpool.** If there are enough computers in a mining pool, the likelihood of at least one of them receiving block rewards is mathematically probable and somewhat predictable. The mining pool operator takes their cut, and then they pay out the remaining benefits equally among the machines involved in the pool.

As I mentioned earlier, in late 2017 the price of BTC started to drop and unfortunately the downward spiral continued into 2018 and beyond. As the Bitcoin price went down, ETH and a bunch of the ALTS (alternative coins) managed to keep going up for a few weeks. But by the end of January 2018, just about everything was going down. And quickly. After topping out just under 20k around December 15, 2017, the price of BTC plummeted to under 9k by February 1, 2018. ETH went from under $300 on 11/5/17 to almost $1300 on 1/11/18 to under $400 by 4/1/18.

These selloffs were just the beginning though. By the end of 2018 the price for one Bitcoin had sunk to under $3,500! As I learned more and more about the 4-

year cycle of Bitcoin, I came to find out that this severe downswing was predicted by tons of people. It was easy to see coming. But for me, that wasn't the case. I didn't sell. I was simply one of the morons who lost their money to the people who knew what they were doing. A retail plebian. A gambling degenerate who lost the same as he always has. A MUSH.

I was prepared to keep playing though. And I was prepared to buy more. During the second half of 2018, as the price of Bitcoin kept getting crushed, I bought more crypto and then in 2019 I bought a bunch more. When I got bonuses from work, I would put the extra cash into Bitcoin and Ethereum. Between late 2018 and 2019 in total we spent another 40k to bolster our crypto stack, with much of our new BTC purchases in the 4k apiece range.

SIDE NOTE: ARE YOU NOTICING A TREND YET WHEN IT COMES TO THE PRICE OF BITCOIN? UP, DOWN, UP, DOWN, UP, DOWN………

All we needed to do now was hodl, the same as we had done during the downswing.

By late 2019 the BTC price had started to climb again. It got to over $10k and approached the $12k mark before retreating back under 10k. I was back to feeling confident.

But as 2020 got started, the covid epidemic came out of nowhere and hit the stock market and the crypto space like a punch to the face. Prices dropped like mad. One BTC went from $10,100 on Feb 18, 2020 to under 5k less than 30 days later. Panic was everywhere in the world, including in crypto. Was BTC going to zero? I didn't think so. So I took out some big loans and proceeded to buy about $80k more in coins. (I told you I am a hardcore gambler.) I bought BTC. I bought ETH. And a boatload of others. And as history shows, I bought them at the right time. We made 5x, 10x, 20x and more on some altcoins when the market rebounded. The BTC price rocketed up to over $60k by the first half of 2021 and the returns on many of the ALTS were just absolutely nutso. At the height of the bubble, we had turned our total investment of approximately $150k cash into a crypto portfolio valued at over $1.1 million.

If you read crypto investment books and articles, you will learn one simple rule: Buy low and sell high. I have learned that when everyone is selling, you should actually be buying. It is so tough to do though. Social media screams with one directive and it is practically impossible to ignore the noise. I stayed invested and even accumulated during some of the selloff periods because of my simple belief in Bitcoin. Long term, Bitcoin is going to win. The technology is superior to what the world has been using and there is a technological shift going on. It is impossible to hold Bitcoin down. Only incredibly bad luck could possibly steal this victory from me. This time I win gambling. And there is more winning to do.

CHAPTER 5: BITCOIN IS THE ANSWER

My wife has been working out lately and she wears this little black outfit when she does the workouts. Tight shorts and a spandex type halter top. I love the look of her. I just followed her into the kitchen to let her know.

"You look so thick and hot right now," I say.

She looks at me with a somewhat confusing sort of stare. "I'm not sure I'm in the mood for sex tonight," she replies.

"Oh that's ok," I respond. "I wasn't really looking to either," I lied. I'd love to have sex with her tonight. Oh well. I have learned not to take things personally as I have gotten older.

Have I mentioned yet that I am divorced twice already?

And remarried a third time. This time successfully. We have been together for more than 9 years now and I am never letting this lady go. That sounds kind of psychotic but I promise you it is not. I am just never going to stop loving her and letting her know that she is special. She is the love of my life and I feel so lucky to have met her. We have children together and a home and we continue to enjoy being around each other. It is a dream come true.

Landing her was admittedly against the odds. 17 year age difference? That's an obvious hurdle. I have always been a good looking guy (starting in my 20's anyway - prior to that I had horrible acne and atrocious hair), but she was 22 when I met her. I was 39 and I was definitely starting to enter the stage of looking older. Plus I had baggage. Two divorces. A child from a previous marriage. Not the most appealing package to some.

Add in the fact that she was in the United States on a J1 visa and that she was only planning to be in the US for 3 months. Work for the summer at the beach. Save some money. Fly back home to Russia.

So what happened? Luck. But then again, in the business world they say that luck is the intersection where preparation meets opportunity. Through the years I got prepared for success in love and I stayed confident while waiting to meet the right woman. I saved money and I bought a house. And perhaps most importantly, I got a puppy. Daisy. A yellow lab that just wanted to play and be rubbed. **INFO:**

Women are defenseless against puppies. At the end of one of our first dates, I can remember asking "So do you want me to take you back to your place or do you want to go see Daisy?"

The answer was simple.

A few months later I asked her another question and the response again was in my favor. We got married a few weeks after that at the local town hall – just the two of us and the Justice of the Peace. And that, as they say in the movies, is all she wrote. Asking a stranger to marry you after knowing them for just a couple of months is usually not a recipe for success, but this time I got lucky. I was prepared and when the opportunity presented itself, I took my shot.

Now it might be time for you to get prepared to take your shot with Bitcoin.

Let's start this crypto section of the chapter by playing a game. Take a guess. How many cryptocurrency coins do you think there are?

Answer: There are more than 20,000 altcoins! And many new ones are being created every day. **INFO: An altcoin is any token, cryptocurrency, or digital asset other than Bitcoin.** Some of the names of these altcoins are NOSHIT, CumRocket, PussyCat, Moby Dick, and Baby Shark. Thousands and thousands of coins, each with a market cap of millions and millions of dollars. And you can bet your ass that some of these are eventually going to become worthless. 100% absolutely worthless. Most of them should really be worthless right now, but at this time in history there is a crazy game of speculation being played by a ton of people who have way too much money. These people want more money, and crazy ass crypto projects have been a way for folks to get next level generational wealth type rich. Come up with an idea, create the project, develop the code, release the coin, and market the ever-living fuck out of it. Then collect the cash from the all too willing to ape all-in masses, and hope and pray that the coin catches on and gains traction. That's pretty much the gameplan for all of these projects.

I didn't know it back then but when I fully started investing in Bitcoin in 2017 I had jumped into the middle of an ICO craze. **INFO: ICO stands for Initial Coin Offering**. An ICO is very similar to an IPO (Initial Price Offering) with the stock market. That's when a stock gets released onto a stock exchange for the first time so that pretty much anyone can buy it. Similarly, an ICO is when a cryptocurrency first gets released to the general public for purchasing.

Once the general public can start to buy a coin, a pyramid truly begins to take shape. **INFO: When I say pyramid here, I mean it in terms of a pyramid scheme.** The founding team, the developers, and the financial backers, who join together to create a project, release a coin in an effort to gain funds to grow their project (and/or make themselves rich). These creators are the base of the pyramid. They create a certain number of coins, grant a chunk to themselves and a chunk to their investors, and then release the rest for sale to the community.

The early members of the community form the next layer of the pyramid. These people usually have some familiarity with the project being launched. Maybe they heard about the tech being developed. Maybe they like the past success of the leadership team. Maybe they know people at an investing hedge fund and they have been told that this particular project is a winner. Maybe they simply follow the Twitter (X) account of the project and look for the level of engagement from followers and the comments that get posted under the project's tweets. Whatever the reason, these coin holders are still early to the party, and they form the second layer of the pyramid scheme. As they accumulate coins, the price starts to rise.

As mentioned, the founders sell to the initial wave of retail investors out of an allocated amount of coins that are specifically designated for sale. This first wave of retail typically gains access to these newly released coins via decentralized exchanges that less "tech savvy" people don't even know exist. **INFO: A decentralized exchange allows for people to trade crypto with one another without going through a middle man.** It is kind of a weeding out period in this way. The people who know what they are doing get in first. As they are buying the price of the coin rises. Nobody is selling at this point. Things are too early. The people who own coins at the beginning stage of a project are waiting for the coin price to jump considerably before they sell.

That is where the next layer of the pyramid enters. The retail plebeians, or plebs – for short. The plebs are the general public, like you and me.

The retail plebs typically gain access to a coin via centralized exchanges. **INFO: A centralized crypto exchange is pretty much a bank for cryptocurrency. You can buy crypto through an exchange. You can hold your crypto in a wallet set up by an exchange. You can trade cryptos on an exchange. And you can sell your crypto on an exchange.** Exchanges make the mass trading of crypto easy. Buyers show up to buy. And sellers are there to sell. This is the marketplace where everything happens. A couple of the most popular exchanges are Binance, Crypto.com, Coinbase and Kraken.

Once a coin gets released to the public via an ICO, the public can choose whether to buy that coin or not. Keep in mind: There are sometimes limiting factors in how to obtain the coin:

1. Different countries have their own crypto laws - you may not be able to buy a certain coin if you live in a certain country. (This would be an example of why someone might use a decentralized exchange. Decentralized exchanges are unregulated and do not need to follow the same laws as regulated exchanges.)

2. There are hundreds of crypto exchanges – Just because a particular crypto is available for sale on one exchange, doesn't mean it is automatically available for sale on another exchange. There is a lengthy process that takes place in order for a coin to get listed on an exchange.

3. There may only be certain trading methods available for acquiring a coin. Consider this: Do you want to spend a particular currency to acquire the coin? Do you want to trade in your Bitcoin to acquire this new coin? Do you want to use ethereum to purchase it? Do you first need to acquire a stable coin in order to buy the coin you want? **INFO: Wikipedia defines stable coins as cryptocurrencies designed to maintain a stable level of purchasing power. Stable coins are often backed in a 1:1 ratio with the US dollar.**

When a new coin gets listed on a centralized exchange, this usually opens up the market to a whole new world of potential buyers (the plebs), and most times that results in a jump in the coin price. People hear about a coin being listed on an exchange. They hear the buzz about the coin. They see the marketing. Maybe they see the price going up and of course they want to get in on the gains. They buy the coin and the price continues to rise. This all makes obvious sense. Increased demand with a fixed supply leads to increased prices. Basic economics. But what most people do not understand is that the "supply" is actually not fixed.

Once retail buyers start to get involved in earnest, this captures the attention of the whales at the base of the pyramid. Prices have gone up to a level where they can now sell their coins and experience some legit gains. Key to this whole scenario is that the whales tend to hold their cryptos in hardware wallets that they control. **INFO: A Ledger and a Trezor are examples of hardware wallets that are extremely popular within the crypto community. A hardware wallet can unplug from the internet so that it cannot be accessed online.** In preparation for their sell order, the whales send their crypto from hardware wallets to the exchange of their choice. In this way, a whole new supply is coming onto the market, and the experts can see it. They can literally see the transaction as it happens because all transactions are recorded in the blockchain. This sparks a run for the exits.

When the whales start to sell, the traders then also start to sell, and there simply is not enough money in the pot to pay everyone out. Prices crash due to limited liquidity, especially with low market cap altcoins.

There is a tremendous difference between the market for Bitcoin and the market for alts. The market cap for Bitcoin is much much higher than it is for Ethereum or any of the other alts. When a whale enters a large sell order for Bitcoin, it is quite possible that there are buyers on the other side just waiting to gobble up some BTC at a reduced price. When a whale sells a large chunk of CumRocket or Moby Dick, there is nobody on the other side thinking it will be a sweet deal to jump into the middle of a firesale. When the gig is up for a small alt, the gig is kinda up. With Bitcoin, the price has always bounced back, and there are strong reasons why:

This is why some people suggest that you should buy Bitcoin immediately, if you haven't already. I am not a salesperson for BTC. I am merely here to get you to consider the option of buying Bitcoin. There are strong cases to be made that the price will continue to go up through time.

The Bitcoin supply is fixed. There will only be 21 million ever created.
The mining for Bitcoin is spread throughout the world.
The Bitcoin network has never been hacked.
Cryptocurrency is gaining acceptance everywhere in the world, day by day.
The richest people in the world are investing in Bitcoin-based projects and infrastructure.

Governments all over the world continue to rack up enormous national debts. These debts will never be paid off. Countries eventually will not have the money to pay the interest on the debt. They will default.

Bitcoin is a hedge against the US dollar and any other money system that is based on debt.
Bitcoin is a bet on superior monetary technology.
Bitcoin is a movement against the powers that be.

Consider joining the cause.

CHAPTER 6: BULL RUNS AND BEAR MARKETS

Here's a question:

What in the heck does my neck injury status and my wife have to do with informing people about the cryptocurrency space? The answer is nothing. I guess I'm writing about my neck injury because I want you to feel bad for me on some level. Or I want you to feel like I must be a real champion for battling through the pain to try to help you people. Honestly, I'm not even sure why I'm putting it in here. Maybe I just don't have anything else to talk about.

And my wife? Well, everyone likes to hear about a hot woman. And a hot Russian woman to boot. But things have changed a little bit through the months as I have been writing this book. When I started writing, Russian women were just flat out hot. Gorgeous. Sexy. And damn that accent is just so captivating.

But as the months of this writing journey have passed, there have been some developments in the world that have added flavor to the subject of a Russian woman. They hail from a country that has attacked a neighbor, Ukraine, and is responsible for thousands and thousands of deaths and an immeasurable amount of suffering. Russia has turned itself into a pariah in the eyes of the western world. But yet I find myself conflicted.

I have been to Russia three times. Each time I was completely blown away with how clean the city streets and parks are. Each time I was blown away with how healthy the people in Russia look. From my estimate, less than ten percent of their people are what I would describe as overweight. The rest are in shape, and they dress much more attractively than the people in the US do. By a longshot. ESPECIALLY the women. The majority of women I have seen are wearing heals and tight pants or nice skirts. Believe me, it is a pleasing experience for a heterosexual male to walk the streets of a Russian city.

Perhaps the most impressive thing I have learned about Russia during the ten plus years of knowing my wife is that the Russian people have a great respect for their elderly. The old people there don't get tossed into nursing homes. They live out their lives in homes with family.

The Russians have free health care. They have free daycare too. Their grocery stores have a small little section of an aisle that is dedicated to cereal. And just a small little piece of that section contains any "sugary" type cereals. There were no Lucky Charms or Fruit Loops or Fruity Pebbles. At least not in the stores I went to. The Russians eat a lot healthier than Americans do. From my perspective, their society does a lot of things better than the Americans do.

On top of all this, I think my mother in law is one of the nicest people I have ever met. She is so caring and optimistic. She dedicated her life to raising her children and she did it in a way that involved a ton of sacrifice.

So how am I supposed to feel? The media in the United States is telling me that Russia is bad. But everything I have seen with my own eyes says that is not the case. Should I allow our children to continue to visit Russia regularly, as they have been doing up until this point in their lives? They love their grandmother and they want to see her. Of course she wants to see them too. But there is a travel advisory for Americans against going to Russia.

Travel advisory be damned. Our kids will be going to Russia to see their grandmother.

As I think about it, the crypto cycles of ups and downs are similar to the ups and downs of my life through the years. Good times followed by bad times. The key for me has been to realize when I am in a good period – like now - and appreciate it as such. Bad times are going to come. That is life. Knowing this allows me to fully appreciate living during the good times. The same can be said for crypto. If you are going to invest in crypto, it is imperative that you truly appreciate the bull runs. So then the question becomes: How do you know when a bull run is starting? It is almost impossible to know. Heck, it is almost impossible to know when you are smack dab in the middle of a crypto bull run; nevermind trying to pinpoint exactly when one is going to begin.

Let's start with a definition. I just typed into google, "what is a crypto bull run" and this is a response I received from Coinbase: "A bull market, or bull run, is defined as a period of time when the majority of investors are buying, demand outweighs supply, market confidence is at a high, and prices are rising."

That is easily understandable. A crypto bull run is an extended period of time when prices are going up. But with crypto, you need to understand that when prices go up, they go up hard core. And then they come down hard core after the bull run is over. So if you don't understand when a bull run is starting, and you don't know when it is going to end, how in the hell are you going to be best positioned to capitalize on things? Here's some help:

The pretty much universally recognized pattern is that crypto runs in four-year price cycles. The four-year crypto cycle runs hand in hand with the Bitcoin halvening cycle. This makes sense. The market is used to operating with a set amount of Bitcoin supply coming onto the market (the newly created Bitcoin supply being earned by miners). And then all of a sudden, one day the amount of mining rewards gets cut in half. Demand stays the same with decreased supply, causing an increase in the BTC price. Yes - technically the supply is not actually decreasing, it is rising at a reduced rate. But the impact on the market is similar.

The last Bitcoin halvening occurred in May 2020, and the next halvening is expected to occur sometime around April of 2024. To try to predict what will happen as we get closer to the 2024 halvening, let's look at the history of the price of Bitcoin before and after previous halvenings:

The first halvening date: **11/28/12**
BTC price on this day: $12.35
BTC price a year later 11/28/13: $1,007.39

The second halvening date: **7/9/16**
BTC price on this day: $650.53
BTC price a year later 7/9/17: $2,506.17

The third halvening date: **5/11/20**
BTC price on this day: $8,821.42
BTC price a year later 5/11/21: $56,612.10

Those are some serious freaking jumps. As we head toward the halvening in 2024, this information will be front and center on the investment talk shows, and every crypto expert in the world will be predicting huge moves to the upside for BTC. There will be a bigtime speculation game being played and the FOMO will be real. This is when the fun could go to the next level.

The Bitcoin network has come a long way since it first was created and the evolution has included many BTC price increases and decreases. Rapid ups and downs. But as time has gone on, it is obvious that the price of a Bitcoin has mostly been in an upward trend. It is the fastest growing asset of all time. I mean, fifteen years ago there wasn't even a thing called Bitcoin. The network has grown year by year and the acceptance of Bitcoin by the existing financial system is growing year by year as well. Yes, there has been pushback, but that pushback is becoming less and less vigorous. As of July 2023, there are multiple bills in the US Congress moving toward trying to legislate the crypto industry and put guardrails in place. Once this happens, ie. once crypto officially becomes fully regulated in the United States, the big financial companies are going to dive into this space with reckless abandon. THERE IS MONEY TO BE MADE FOR THEM. And if cryptocurrency is going to impact their existing business ecosystem, you can bet that the largest financial companies in the world are going to want to profit from it.

SIDE NOTE: YES I SOUND LIKE A SALESPERSON. SORRY. THERE ARE JUST SO MANY SIGNS THAT THE PRICE OF BITCOIN IS HEADED HIGHER AND HIGHER.

On top of that, there are already companies outside of the financial vertical that have adopted a pro Bitcoin stance (Microstrategy owns more than 150,000 Bitcoin), and many other companies will likely jump into it as well. As Bitcoin continues to grow, the entire crypto system will grow. And it is my prediction that at some point there will be a "shortage" of Bitcoin. As of July 2023, 63% of the entire Bitcoin supply has been "dormant" for over a year, meaning that 63% of all Bitcoin ever produced has just sat in a wallet for the past year. Even more interestingly, 44% of all Bitcoin hasn't moved from a wallet since September of 2018. That's almost five years. People owning these Bitcoins are either hardcore HODLers or those Bitcoin have been lost.

Let's dig further into the numbers: Roughly 95% of the 21 million Bitcoin that can ever be mined have already been mined. For simple math purposes, let's round off and say 20 million Bitcoin has already been mined. That means roughly 8.8 million Bitcoin haven't moved wallet addresses in at least 5 years. It is highly likely that those Bitcoin will not be moving in the near future either. When the Bitcoin stampede happens, the supply available for sale is going to get very tight, very quick. In my opinion, that will kick off a bull run of historical proportions.

And then, just as everything is steamrolling upwards, things will come to a screeching halt. Some piece of news will hit the airwaves, and the selling will begin. The bull market will turn to a bear market overnight. So what should you do?

The data would seem to suggest that you should buy just prior to the halvening. And sell 6-12 months afterward.

CHAPTER 7: GET UP

"What the fuck was that?" I thought to myself as I struggled to maintain my balance. I looked around to see who had blindsided me and locked eyes with a dude standing about 15 feet away. "He did that on purpose," I concluded as I decided what to do next. We were in the last two minutes of our men's league basketball game. Our team was losing by a few points, but that didn't matter right now. My adrenaline had spiked and I needed to defend myself against this turd who had cheap shot me with a body check out of nowhere.

"What the fuck was that?" I said out loud this time as I rapidly approached the obvious culprit. I didn't see him do it, but he was staring me down so it seemed obvious that this guy who I had never seen play before must have been the guy who did it.

"What's your problem?" I said angrily as I stepped right up into his airspace. Things escalated quickly from there. He put his right hand up into my face and as I went to knock it away, he put his fingers into my left eye, knocking my contact lens out. My eyesight blurred immediately. Something hit me on the left side of my face and I staggered backward, trying to protect myself. I could see blurry figures (other players) to my right but I was unable to see anything to my left, so I focused on backing up to get away from being hit again. I had no clue how to defend myself in this situation though. As I moved backward, the dude charged and swung with a vengeance. I was sent hurtling to the ground by a blow. I was 45 years old and this was the first time in my life that I had been punched in the face.

After a few seconds on the ground, I got to my feet, took out my other contact lens, and looked around. More chaos ensued, but we can leave the rest of the story for another day. My point here has been made. I have had my ass kicked. And I got back up.

Let's start this chapter at a specific date: May 12th, 2022. The crypto world is ablaze, and not in a good way. One of the top crypto projects has gone kaput, and it is taking the entire crypto market down with it. LUNA, the central coin of the Terra blockchain protocol, which had topped out around $116 a coin on April 4, 2022 is today worth less than a fraction of a cent – less than $.0006 to be exact.

What a collapse! LUNA had moved into the top 5 largest projects as recently as April of 2022 with a total market cap in excess of $40 billion……but today, about a month later, it is essentially worthless. Why did this happen? The straightforward and short reason is because most cryptos are a scam. The developers, the creators, the institutional backers who provide the upfront cash to get everything started – they all made their money. Yes they lost a chunk when it crashed, but there is no reason to feel bad for them. It is the retail chumps who take it in the proverbial brown eye on this one. **INFO: brown eye means the ass.** The whole situation is disgusting. And I didn't even have any money in LUNA. I lost nothing from it - Except the accompanying collapse in the price of Bitcoin and other cryptos that I do own whose prices have been affected. BTC had gone from $45k on May 1st to under $29k by May 12. I took a loss, yes, but not a 99.9% loss within a day.

Imagine having bought LUNA in June of 2020 with an entry cost that was roughly 20 cents per coin. OMG! What a win! Life changing in so many ways. But what if you didn't get in that early? Heck, what if you had simply bought in at $10 in July of 2021 and rode it up to $120 less than a year later? Let's say you invested $10,000 into LUNA at $10 per coin - that means you would have made $110,000 when the coin rose up to $120 apiece! Sounds pretty great to me. I would be walking around feeling like a champ, prepared to give my sound financial advice to anyone who might even think about asking for it.

Now try to put yourself in the shoes of the people who bought LUNA at $0.20 and think about how many times their money increased. $10,000 worth of LUNA bought at $0.20 would have netted them $6 million! Yes, I'm sure they would have cashed out some during the run (unless they were a more hardcore gambler than I am). They probably bought some nice things (Lamborghinis, a mansion, lots of prostitutes and drugs) but I'm sure they also left a chunk of their stack in the market because they thought LUNA was going to continue going up. Why wouldn't that be the way they think? It had gone from 20 cents to $120 apiece in less than two years. Why should it stop at $120? Then the next day they see that LUNA is now worthless. One whale sells. Another whale sells. And another and another. Then retail sells once the news breaks that the project is crashing to the ground. Get out while you can. Luna is down to zero in a matter of hours.

SIDE NOTE: CAPITALIZING ON WINNING TRADES IS A MUST IN CRYPTO. IT IS EASY TO MAKE MONEY DURING BULL RUNS, BUT IF YOU DON'T CASH ANYTHING OUT DURING HIGH POINTS, YOU SIMPLY LOSE IT ALL BACK DURING THE BEAR MARKETS. I FEEL LIKE I SHOULD SAY THAT HERE. IT IS A RANDOM THOUGHT, BUT IT IS DEFINITELY 100% TRUE. YOU MUST FIND A WAY TO CASH OUT WHILE THINGS ARE GOING IN A POSITIVE DIRECTION. I'M NOT REALLY THE BEST AT IT, TO BE HONEST WITH YOU. OUR ONE-TIME CRYPTO STACK OF OVER $1 MILLION IS NOW DOWN TO UNDER $500,000.

It is imperative to understand that whatever coins we own can all go crashing down to zero, and there are many reasons why it can happen. There could be a security hack. There could be a developer issue that shuts down the network. There could be a huge selloff by a whale that sparks a selloff by retail that just keeps moving the price of the coin lower and lower and lower. We can lose it all at any point. And the fear of losing 100% of your investment overnight should be particularly elevated for anyone investing in crypto. Why? Because the majority of us don't have a clue about how these technologies actually work! Only the hardcore nerds know how this stuff works. These hardcore nerds (and the friends and business associates of hardcore nerds) have an obvious advantage when it comes to predicting the success of a project, and therefore the success of coins tied to that project.

Even more importantly, there are people who completely understand the trading systems for these coins. They know the ins and the outs of trading on exchanges. And because they understand these nuances, they control the market. These whales control huge amounts of coins. And they know that they can single-handedly impact the price of the coins that they own. How? Leverage.

The marketplace for trading crypto allows people to bet that the price of a coin is going to go up or down. Not only can you bet on which direction it is going to go, but you can also use leverage to supercharge your wager. It is possible to trade using 2x, 5x, 10x, 50x or even 100x leverage! I'm not going to go into a huge explanation of how trading with leverage works, but a brief way to describe it would be that if you want to trade one dollar worth of a coin and you do it with 10x leverage, the coin price can only go down ten cents before you are broke and your trade is closed. If the coin goes up 10 cents, you will have doubled your money to two dollars. Using 20x leverage in this example means the coin can only go down 5 cents before you are broke, and if it goes up 10 cents you would now be up to three dollars (200% profit).

The key to leveraged trading is knowing when to long trade (bet the price will go up) vs when to short trade (bet the price will go down). And if you possess enough coins or cash, you can single-handedly drive the market in the direction of your choice.

INFO: When traders have a winning trade in crypto, they actually get paid their winnings in the crypto they are trading in. When whales make a leveraged trade shorting Bitcoin, if Bitcoin goes down, they actually get paid the proceeds of their winning trade in Bitcoin! This is how traders acquire more Bitcoin as prices go down!

Here's an example: Let's say that the price of Bitcoin has been steadily rising for a couple of days and there are lots of open Bitcoin leveraged long trades that are in the positive. People are winning the trades, but they are leaving the trades open because they think the price is going to continue to move higher. A whale sees all of these open trades, and he initiates a leveraged short position. He then moves a huge stack of his coins onto an exchange and proceeds to immediately sell those coins. As I mentioned earlier, this causes the coin price to drop. Because other traders see this happening in real time, they close out (or get liquidated) their leveraged long trades, which causes the coin price to drop more. As the selling continues, the whale who made the leveraged short trade is gaining huge amounts of Bitcoin. The whale closes out their short trade and then the market resets with the whale simply holding onto their BTC. They let the price rise over the following days or weeks or months and then they do the same thing all over again. The whales work in a team this way to screw the little guy.

Yes, this is an oversimplified example. But the core of it is 100% accurate. When people trade Bitcoin on exchanges, whether they bet the price is going up or down, they are trading against people who are betting that the coin price will move in the opposite direction. When you leverage trade betting that the price of a coin will go up, more and more people need to be buying the coin in order for your trade to keep winning. It is simple math. If there are many more open long trades in the system, the whales will short, and then sell their stack so that they can clear those long trades out. And if the whales are betting long, they usually are doing so because they see a bunch of open short trades. The key here: The whales have the stacks to move the market.

So we then need to ask: WHO ARE THE WHALES?

CHAPTER 8: CRYPTO COMMON SENSE

Recently I went to a local casino with a couple of friends. One of those friends got into buying crypto a couple of years ago, somewhat near the top of the market in 2021. He is no longer a fan of crypto.

"I just want to get as much of what I had, sell it all, and never be involved with the stuff again," he said to me during the ride to the casino.

I pondered my response. The time to get out was a year ago when things were flying high. Not now when things are at the bottom. He had invested about ten thousand dollars and built the stack up to somewhere around 25k in value before things toppled. He cashed nothing out and his total crypto stack in late 2022 was less than what he had originally put in. He had lost money, so I felt bad. But the truth still came out of my mouth.

"That's good for me. I don't like to say it, but if that is how lots of people are feeling, that's when prices start to rise. After the small people all get crushed, prices go back up and the whole process happens again."

He didn't care for my response. I wouldn't have liked my response either if I was him. I did my best to explain that now is exactly the WRONG time to be selling but my words were not convincing enough, apparently. He is done with crypto. As are plenty of other people. That's ok. I have my own things I need to worry about right now.

The year is 2022 and we are in the middle of a bear market for crypto. The hodl strategy hasn't been working out too great for me lately as the price of one Bitcoin is down to under $18k vs the highs of over $63k in 2021. Our one time stack of over a million US dollars is now down to 400k. I have 300k in loans that I took out to buy the crypto though, so we are only actually "up" about 100k.

The prices of cryptos are going to bounce back. I am positive of that. It's only a matter of time. But our savings is starting to run low. And my wife is starting to ask questions.

"I thought we were millionaires?"

"We were," I replied. "I thought it was gonna stay that way. But we will be again. It's just gonna take some time. We need to stay patient."

"The flights to Russia are going to cost over $5,000. And we will need spending money when we get there. This trip isn't going to be cheap."

My wife quit her job earlier this year. I think she might be feeling a pinch in her savings. We have always kept our finances separate since we have been married. I pay all the bills. The groceries each week. The cars. Insurance. The mortgage. Vacations. Christmas presents. Just about everything. She pitches in here and there but for the most part she only spends money on things she wants for herself and extra stuff for the kids. I kinda like it this way. I like being the provider. But what I don't particularly like is the direction that this conversation is heading.

"I understand," I responded. "Just relax. We have the money to pay for the trip. I will venmo you the cash."

"Please don't tell me to relax," she replied while raising her voice. "You told me we were rich and that I didn't need to worry about money. Now today you are telling me to watch how much I spend while visiting my family for the first time in three years. Which is it?"

"Both," I told her. "Things are just getting a little tight. I'm not working and we are eating into our savings. I could sell some of our Bitcoin, but I don't want to. Now is when we should be buying. I just-"

"You always think that!" she interrupted. "This affects me too, you know. We both agreed last year that I could quit my job. You said we would be fine. Now I want to go see my mother for the first time in three years and you are making it seem like we don't have the money."

"I just told you we have the money. I said I will venmo it to you."

This isn't going at all how I wanted it to go. Yes, the fact is that money is starting to get tight. Most of our cash is invested into crypto. The savings we do have in cash is being eaten into slowly but surely each month. I have been gambling a bit more than I should have. And I've been losing.

I never say anything about money. I just pay. The one time I do say something, we have a problem.

"I don't want to argue." My wife is speaking a bit more calmly now. "I just want to know what's going on."

We sit down together over the next 60 minutes and I show her exactly what we have in our savings and in our crypto investment accounts. We mutually decide that I will stay home and watch the dog while she and the kids go to Russia. This will save a couple thousand bucks. Plus, when I am in Russia I stand out like a sore thumb as an American. I'm like at least 6 inches taller than everyone over there. And I only speak English. Add all that together and it's probably not the best idea for me to go. We also mutually agree that we will open a joint bank account to use for our family finances moving forward.

There are groups of people actively hunting your Bitcoin every single day. They want it. And their plan is for you to willingly give it to them. They bring their own deck of cards to the card game. They deal the cards and they are really good at it. You are not able to see them dealing from the bottom of the deck until you are flat out broke. And then there is nothing you can do about it.

In this chapter I will dive into the group of people I refer to as whales. For the most part, these whales are members of the communities of miners, exchanges and traders who control everything within the crypto world. They have controlled everything from the beginning. Crypto is a game they are not going to lose, because this relatively small group of people control vast amounts of Bitcoin.

In order to analyze how the crypto market works, let's take a look at history and use some common sense. Pretend we are back in 2009 when Bitcoin was first invented. You and me are running the Bitcoin software on our computers; we are mining Bitcoin! Our computers are solving blocks and earning rewards. Lots of it. 50 BTC per block. At this time, Bitcoin is completely worthless, but we are hard core techies and we love playing with cutting edge software. This Bitcoin stuff seems so cool. We get horny at the sound of it.

Our pretend story continues the following year (2010) when Laszlo pays for his pizzas in Bitcoin. That's when Bitcoin officially starts to have value. And that's when crypto officially becomes about money and power.

The years go by and more people begin mining. We are no longer being rewarded with as much BTC as before, so we invent high powered specialized supercomputers to better mine BTC. This is where our story gets interesting.

This new mining equipment is far superior to what other people are using and we begin earning large amounts of BTC again. But there is more. We come to the realization that we can sell these Bitcoin superminers to other people and make a ton of money.

And that's the end of our pretend story. You and me didn't invent Bitcoin superminers. Someone else did.

SIDE NOTE: IF YOU HAVEN'T FIGURED IT OUT YET, THE POINT OF OUR PRETEND STORY IS TO RECOGNIZE THAT THE PEOPLE WHO GOT INTO MINING BITCOIN EARLY ON ARE THE SAME PEOPLE WHO CONTROL THE MARKET NOWADAYS. THEY ARE THE ONES WHO HOLD LOTS OF COINS BECAUSE THEY GOT INTO THE SPACE AND ACCUMULATED BITCOIN BACK WHEN IT WAS WORTHLESS. AND THEN THEY HELPED TO BUILD OUT THE ENTIRE CRYPTO ECOSYSTEM.

As Bitmain (founded in China back in 2013) begins to mass produce its' Antminers, they realize that there are a number of different ways for them to increase the amount of Bitcoin they can earn. Here is one way that is not often talked about:

Before any of the Antminers are actually sold, they first need to be tested to make sure they work correctly. As they are being tested, they are generating more and more Bitcoin for Bitmain…………..Thousands of the very best, fastest Bitcoin miners all running and sending their solved mining block rewards to the Bitmain wallet. Maybe Bitmain tests the miners for a couple of days. Maybe a couple of weeks. Maybe months. Whatever the case, they are making money (BTC) before they even sell and ship the machines to their customers!

Bitmain developed the strongest Bitcoin miners. They then used those miners to accumulate a ton of Bitcoin for themselves. Then they resold the units to an eagerly awaiting public for a nice profit. You might ask: What did they do with all those profits?

In 2014, Bitmain launches Antpool, a mining pool operation (based in China) that grows to be one of the largest in the world. **INFO: In 2016, Bitmain acquires BTC.com which is also one of the largest Bitcoin mining operations in the world.** On a side note, F2Pool, a mining pool that is well known for manipulating the price of Bitcoin, is also based in China. Together these three mining pools mine more than 50% of the total Bitcoin created for a number of years. When mining

CHAPTER 10: SATOSHI IS A GENIUS

And on come the blue lights.

"Fuck," I say to myself as I pull the car over. I was doing 50 or so in a 35 mph zone. Not crazy fast, but fast enough to get a ticket.

"License and Registration," the officer says as he approaches my open car window.

"Yes sir," I respond. I lean over to grab the registration out of the glove box. Luckily the car did not smell like pot. It was early in the day, and I hadn't gotten around to smoking yet.

"Where are you headed?" he asked.

"I have a meeting for a tv show that I am trying to make. Sorry I was driving a little too fast."

"What kind of tv show?"

"I'm trying to make the world a better place. There is just so much bad stuff going on. I want to try to get more good stuff on tv for people to think about. If you want to read about it, I can give you a paper I have written."

"OK let me take a look," he replied. I was 21 years old and I was nervous – probably more nervous about his opinion on the paper than I was about getting a ticket. I handed him my flyer. He took it, along with my license and registration, and headed back to his vehicle with the flashing lights.

The year was 1995. Here is what was on that paper:

Help Eliminate America's PERMANENT HAZE

This could be the most important letter you read in your life. My name is (Name Withheld) and my goal is to help as many people as possible. I want to lessen the violence and hatred that is so prominent in American society.

Let me start by asking everyone to read carefully every word written here. Please don't just glance over the words and then throw out the paper. I have a plan to eliminate some of the problems that exist today, but I need help. Many

a coincidence. The most important thing that I have learned is going to be explained in detail in the next chapter. This is incredibly random and completely out of nowhere, but that's how things happen in life. Bad things. Out of nowhere. Never saw it coming. Well…..I'm trying to give you a heads up for sometime in the future. Something bad is coming.

Here is the crazy and awesome part about the BCH hard fork: When it happened, anyone who owned Bitcoin was automatically credited with an exact same amount of Bitcoin Cash units.

Unsurprisingly, Bitmain and the China based miners were heavily in favor of the Bitcoin Cash split. Upon the completion of the hard fork, these organizations got credited with lots and lots of BCH. Free money! One BCH for every BTC they owned. They then set about making the value of their "free" BCH go up. And that's where the Antminers needing to be paid for in BCH comes into play.

When Bitmain required people to buy Antminers using Bitcoin Cash, they were helping to increase the value of their BCH coins. In order to obtain BCH to make an Antminer purchase, people all over the world would need to deposit their cash (or other cryptos) into an exchange (like Binance – which was founded in July of 2017 – one month before the bitcoin cash hard fork!) to buy BCH. Then the people would send the BCH to Bitmain to purchase the Antminer. This gave BCH a special form of value, helping the price of 1 BCH to rise from **$225 in August of 2017 to almost $4,000 US dollars by December of 2017!** Come December of 2018, the price for 1 BCH was back under $200. Do you think that Binance and Bitmain and the Chinese mining pools sold plenty of their freely acquired BCH on the open market when the price was at its' highest? Yes. Yes, they did. These people are expert traders!

To summarize: The whales own the coins, and they make the rules. They control the mining of Bitcoin. They control the exchanges. And they know how to trade to take your money. They work together to aggressively fuck your financial investments in every reachable orifice. And they don't use lubricant. Everything is coordinated. Everything is intentional. It is the definition of a rigged game. And it would be funny if it wasn't so damned deadly serious.

The whales are always in control of the price of coins. When they want things to go up, prices go up. When they want prices to come down, they come down. The whales pull all of the strings from behind the curtain and most crypto investors have no clue that they are being completely manipulated. That pisses me off.

There are patterns to crypto. The same things keep happening over and over again. I have been watching it play out for more than seven years now. I've noticed trends and I have also noticed things occur that just absolutely cannot be pools are awarded coins, they eventually need to sell some of those coins to pay for their operating expenses. They need relationships with exchanges to complete those sales.

Enter Binance. Binance, founded in 2017 in China, by Changpeng Zhao, (who was born in China and moved to Canada when he was 12 years old), became the largest crypto exchange in the world by trading volume by April 2018. **INFO: You read that correctly. Within one year they grew to be the largest crypto exchange in the world. Wow that was fast.**

While this is happening, CZ Binance, as Changpeng Zhao becomes known, essentially becomes the king of crypto. He proceeds to lead Binance through years of explosive growth and sets the standard for crypto trading throughout the world. By May of 2023, it is estimated that Binance is responsible for 70% of trades for the entire crypto market.

SIDE NOTE: BINANCE IS HEAVILY INVOLVED IN JUST ABOUT EVERY FACET OF THE CRYPTO SUPPLY CHAIN. THIS GIVES THEM INCREDIBLE POWER OVER THE ENTIRE INDUSTRY. AND THEY CAN USE THIS POWER TO PRETTY MUCH CREATE THEIR OWN RULES.

Let's now consider something that I wrote about back in chapter 3. Remember when I mentioned that people had to use Bitcoin Cash (BCH is the coin ticker) to pay for their Antminers from Bitmain? I bought the used Antminer through Amazon back in 2017 because I didn't want to wait for a new one to be shipped to me from China, and also because I was a little confused as to why I would have to pay for the Antminer using Bitcoin Cash. It just seemed strange to me at the time. But it makes perfect sense to me now.

On August 1, 2017, there was a "hard fork" of the Bitcoin network. **INFO: A hard fork happens when a group of developers make changes to a project's blockchain.** Back in 2017, there was a group of people who felt that in order for Bitcoin to scale most effectively, the Bitcoin network would need to process transactions much more quickly than it was capable of at the time. In an attempt to fix this "problem", these people created a new strain of Bitcoin, with many of the same qualities of the original, and they termed it Bitcoin Cash. They created a new coin (BCH) and developed the software that essentially "forked off" from the Bitcoin blockchain, thus creating their own new blockchain.

of my friends have volunteered but we need help from everyone else with a caring heart. Here is the plan. We are putting together a show made for television that will deal with issues that effect people and how we can make a difference. The show will be called Permanent Haze. The long term plan for Permanent Haze will be to get money from advertisements, commercials, and promotions. All of this money raised by the show will go toward rebuilding schools, neighborhoods, and churches in American cities and suburbs.

The best part of this plan is that there are no bad side effects. Also, there does not need to be much effort made by anyone but my friends and me. The only thing that we ask is for people to watch their television once a week, something everyone does already. If we can get one out of every twenty Americans to watch Permanent Haze, we will be able to do a lot of good for the country.

Many people often say that they would like to help solve the problems of today, but they just don't know where to start. There is simply too much to do, they say. We are giving everyone a starting point right now. The first step in this process is complete because you have read this paper. Now we need you to tell as many people as possible about the idea. Make copies of this page and pass them around to your friends and coworkers. Tell them to do the same. Then, when Permanent Haze comes on, watch it. We will do the rest, but we just need a little support from everyone.

If you would like to help even more, you can call your local newspaper and tell them about this idea. Let's get as much publicity focused on this as possible. If we do not try to change things, society will continue to get worse. Look around. Look at today's newspapers. Watch the news. My friends and I do not want all of this violence to continue and we don't think most other people do either. Let's do something about it. Let's quit being lazy and try to help for once. It will not take much effort.

Here are the facts. This idea is possible. This does make sense. All we need is a small amount of effort from people who want to do good. Please help by doing what we ask. Thank you very much. Remember, reading this was only the first step in the process.

(Name Withheld)

Wow I was a naïve 21-year-old. Things never went anywhere with Permanent Haze. You probably already guessed that lol. I gave some effort, but I didn't have the right contacts and I didn't do a good job of plowing through the obstacles that came up along the way. If you want to change the world, you need to have a bit more dedication and determination than I had at the time. Plus, if I'm being honest, I wasn't that good of a writer back then. This paper kinda sucked.

On the positive side of things, that cop came back to my car and gave me back my license and let me go with a warning.

This chapter will not be pleasant. It will be scary.

I have a warning for you: The United States is at war with China. And China WILL win if we continue down the path we are on. Their weapon of choice to deliver the final blow? Bitcoin. This is why I decided to write this book. And it is also why I have chosen to remain anonymous. The powers behind the curtain do not want this information in the hands of regular everyday citizens.

Earlier in the book, I wrote that nobody knows who Satoshi Nakamoto is. That was a lie. I do.

The Chinese government is Satoshi Nakamoto. They created bitcoin and day by day they have been successfully executing a plan to grow bitcoin into a sprawling array of cryptos. They use that network of cryptocurrencies to take more and more money from greedy Americans. Sure, some Americans have made huge gains from crypto, but so so so many others have gotten crushed. At the same time, plenty of China's people have entirely changed their standard of living due to crypto. Chinese citizens who bought Antminers and used the free government supplied power to mine Bitcoin probably made out pretty good through time as the price of BTC grew to 65k US DOLLARS in 2021, right?

The whales have crushed the retail public time and time again. When things get too hot, the whales sell and bring prices back down to earth, pocketing additional BTC via short trades in the process. Each time, the dumb retail public has no idea what hit them. THE WHALES CONTROL THE MARKET BECAUSE THEY HAVE MOST OF THE COINS! The Antminer was invented and manufactured in China by a Chinese company. The world's largest exchange, Binance, was founded in China.

The largest mining farms for many years have been based in China. The same people own these companies. DOESN'T THAT SOUND SUSPICIOUS TO YOU?

Many of the bigtime whales controlling everything are from China. Use your brain.

How did China know to get into crypto earlier than everyone else in the world? Was it just a lucky bet? No. They have a plan. This plan involves keeping the creator of Bitcoin anonymous. If the Americans ever knew Bitcoin was invented by China, there is no way the American government would allow people to buy it, especially knowing that there is over 1 million Bitcoin sitting in Satoshi's wallets, untouched. If this is all true, that means the Chinese could completely mess with the entire crypto market at any time they wish.....

And that is what eventually will happen. The Satoshi coins will be used as a weapon. This weapon will deliver the death blow to the financial control that the United States holds over other countries.

SIDE NOTE: THIS IS NOT A CRAZY PREDICTION. IT IS LITERALLY EXACTLY WHAT THEY DID TO TAKE DOWN FTX. MORE ON THAT IN AN UPCOMING CHAPTER...

It has been a long and complicated process, but phase 1 of the plan is almost complete: Get the Western world to embrace Bitcoin. Here's how they did it:

China began the attack in 2009 by revealing and unleashing the base model of blockchain technology for the financial sector – Bitcoin - one of the greatest inventions in the history of mankind. While the Bitcoin network slowly gained users between 2009-2013, exactly half of the total supply of Bitcoin that will ever be created was released onto the market. 10.5 million BTC. Satoshi and his contacts mined the lion's share of these coins. Of course, they did! They were the only people in the world who knew about it! The early bird gets the Bitcoin in this case.

With the help of Bitmain, China controlled the mining for the Bitcoin network through the stage of growth years from 2013-2021, with Chinese companies mining the majority of the BTC. During the years 2016-2019, it is estimated that China mined between 65-75% of the world's yearly mined Bitcoin, and Bitmain's Antminers were at the center of the production.

As the Bitcoin network grew, China mined so much of the world's Bitcoin that some people in the industry came to fear a 51% attack. **Info: A 51% attack in crypto refers to a network being able to fork to something different because more than 51% of the network powering devices get programmed to follow the new fork.** To clarify: People used to fear a 51% attack. They don't anymore. In 2021 the country of China outlawed Bitcoin mining. Hmmmm. Interesting. They absolutely controlled the mining market for all of Bitcoin's history up until that point, but then they suddenly decided to stop when the price was more than $45,000 US dollars for one Bitcoin? That doesn't make much sense.

What people don't know is that China didn't want the world to fear a 51% attack. And they especially didn't want the regulators and politicians in the United States to fear a 51% attack. If that possibility got played up in the news media, the politicians most certainly would not be suggesting an American embrace of Bitcoin.

A large increase in the percentage of American mining operations takes place during the next couple of years after mining is outlawed in China in 2021. By the year 2023, it is estimated that more than 60% of all the world's mining is now done in the US. No more fears of a 51% attack. And the American governing body and financial community are responding as planned. Bitcoin is NOT a security. This has been decided on by the US government. That essentially means it is legal to invest in it without having to worry about new regulations coming from the politicians.

Here is my message to you: When an imaginary piece of internet money rises to being worth $30,000 (July of 2023), there are plenty of investors looking to get involved. No less than 8 Bitcoin ETF (Exchange Traded Fund) applications are in front of the SEC (Securities and Exchange Commission) as of August 2023, led by one from investment giant Black Rock. When these ETF applications ultimately get approved – and they will get approved – the Bitcoin gold rush will begin. The price of Bitcoin will go up. And the Fear Of Missing Out will be real. Bitcoin will be a "must own" asset.

Satoshi Nakamoto is smarter than you and I. Bit by bit, deeper and deeper – like a tick – he (they) planned for Bitcoin to inject itself into the US financial system, an easy target if ever there was one. The great wealth of the United States is based on debt. A debt that is growing more and more each year. A debt that realistically can never be paid back. As entitlements grow, Social Security, Medicare and interest on the debt will eventually comprise too large of a total expense compared to the taxes that are collected. The house of cards, debt based financial system of the fiat world will start to collapse and the dollar will lose its' purchasing power.

I will remind you that Satoshi told us how he felt about the financial system in his original mined block of Bitcoin: "The Times 03/Jan/2009 Chancellor on brink of second bailout for banks."

The country with the strongest financial system has the most money to create the best military weapons. For decades the United States of America has spent the most amount of money on defense. We spend more than most other countries combined. As a result, the US has the strongest arsenal of weapons in the world. Do you think China likes that? No. No they do not. But China has no interest in a military fight right now. They would lose the fight and they know it. There has to be another way...

Don't attack the US physically. Instead, weaken the society with drugs (fentanyl). Destroy the national pride of the US using social media (TikTok – ironic that is the name of the social media app from China, isn't it? Almost like there is a countdown going on.). Infiltrate the financial system. The Americans are rich and greedy. They will embrace their own demise.

Satoshi really is a genius.

CHAPTER 11: LINGCHI

Bzzzzzzzzzz. Bzzzzzzzzzz. Bzzzzzzzzzzzzzzzzzzzz. It's tough cutting my hair like this. Nobody else around to help me or at least tell me if I'm missing any part. I'm going right down to the scalp with the clippers. Skinhead style. I haven't done this haircut in 15 years, at least. Just felt like today would be a good day to do it. It's the middle of summer and it is time for a change. This will help me keep cool. And maybe most importantly, my wife and kids left on a plane for Russia today. If I look stupid with a bald head at least I will be the only one around who has to look at it. Still, I do hope that I don't miss any spots in the back...

Dropping the family off at the airport was tough. I had to hold in my crying because I didn't want to make the kids cry. They were obviously sad. I held a long embrace with each of the kids, smiled and said "Be good for Mom!" as they turned and headed toward the check in area to begin their journey. Two flights and 26 hours later they would be landing at their destination in Russia, hugging my mother-in-law and other family members and friends. I will be home solo until they return in 24 days.

24 days to myself. What will I do? Watch the dog, for one. So I guess that technically means I won't be by myself. But I can stash her at the dog boarding place when I have things to do. I'm definitely going to Saratoga at least once. That's my favorite place in the world. Saratoga Race Track in Saratoga Springs, NY. The people there are nice. The horses are spectacularly beautiful animals. The gambling is great. And the women in Saratoga come dressed to impress!

Besides Saratoga, I have no plans as of yet. I'm sure I will go sing karaoke a few times. There has been talk of a group trip to Las Vegas within my circle of friends in a couple of weekends. Not sure if that will happen, but if it does, that would be cool. Whatever. The world is my oyster. I have a shaved head and I'm ready to enjoy some time with no responsibilities.

I could start this chapter with a discussion about Chinese made fentanyl that has been pouring across the borders of the United States, killing tens of thousands of Americans every year. In case you didn't know, fentanyl is the leading cause of death for Americans between the ages of 18-45. Or I could talk about TikTok and how the Chinese are collecting data on the young people in the USA. Data that they are using to target us now - and will use to target us in the future. I could also talk about how Chinese companies and individuals are buying up farmland in the United States like crazy. But let's not focus on any of these facts right now. Let's talk about something else instead.

Let's talk about COVID 19. I know. I know. You're all talked out about covid 19. But please bear with me.

Remember the stories about the scientists that all worked in Wuhan and got sick and had to be hospitalized? As The Wall St Journal put it in their July 20, 2023 edition: "A prominent scientist who worked on coronavirus projects funded by the US government is one of three Chinese researchers who became sick with an unspecified illness during the initial outbreak of covid 19...." #NotaCoincidence

Then we had the doctor from Wuhan Central Hospital who tried to warn the public during the early days of the covid virus but was stopped by the Chinese government. Dr Li Wenliang was his name. Look him up if you don't believe me. China wanted to hide this thing. And they wanted everyone to be scared. Mission accomplished.

Remember when we first heard about coronavirus here in the US back in January of 2020? Remember seeing the videos on social media of people in China walking along and then just collapsing dead on the streets? That was the coronavirus. That's what we were told. So we were naturally all scared as hell because people were walking down the street collapsing dead. We had no idea what it was. We had no idea what was coming here. Of course we were all scared! We should have been. But so many of us are still scared today. Way too many! It seems like all you idiots out there are still petrified. The people who wear a mask while alone in their car give me a particularly energized frustration level.

We have allowed China to completely damage our morale as a country. Our psyche as a country. Everything we know now seems different....and a big chunk of it is because of the coronavirus and the reactions by the government of the United States. Two weeks to stop the spread. Remember that? Donald Trump, Mike Pence, Anthony Fauci. They had no clue what they were talking about. They were just trying to get us to lock down because they wanted to get control over the situation. But in the end, they had no control. And also in the end, it probably cost Donald Trump the 2020 election. Some might say this is the main reason why the coronavirus was intentionally released....but I digress........

China did this all to us intentionally. It is why they were researching these diseases (well maybe they were researching them because the US was giving them money to do so....). It's why they were messing with the DNA of these diseases. Messing around with gain of function or whatever the fuck you want to call it. They were experimenting with viruses. And why would they do that?

SIDE NOTE: IF YOU DON'T THINK THAT THE ANSWER IS TO USE IT AS A WEAPON, THEN YOU ARE NOT SMART AND YOU MAY AS WELL JUST STOP READING RIGHT NOW.

Why am I so sure that China released covid intentionally? Well for one, all of the facts show that is the case. There was a working lab right down the road from where the virus was supposedly created in the wet market. You morons! What's the likelihood of that? Planet earth is this huge freakin place, and there's a high level lab (the Wuhan Institute of Virology, where the world's foremost bat researcher worked) right down the road from where this virus just happened to first begin? A statistical improbability, to say the least. Then add in that China hid the fact that there was an extremely potent virus circulating amongst its population. They bought up extra healthcare supplies (masks, gowns, etc) from the US and other countries, leaving those countries short of those supplies when the virus fully broke out in those areas of the world. China knew what was happening. They shut down travel within their borders. All flights inside of China were canceled. But they let international flights keep going. They shipped the virus all over the world. Intentionally. Why wouldn't they shut down all travel to help contain the virus? Why wouldn't they do that? Because they didn't want to be blamed for starting it.

Make no mistake about it, China did this because they had a long term vision and a long term plan for how to defeat, dethrone, and destroy the United States. They are carrying out the plan step by meticulous step. And we have idiots in this country who think oh no no no, that's not what's going on here. **What more needs to happen for you to understand that we're in the middle of a war**? China is hitting us from all angles and they are somehow doing this without arousing suspicion from the mainstream community in the United States. This is the ultimate form of Lingchi. (Wikipedia defines Lingchi as Death By a Thousand Cuts – a form of torture and execution used in China from roughly 900 AD up until the practice ended around the early 1900's. In this form of execution, a knife was used to methodically remove portions of the body over an extended period of time, eventually resulting in death.)

The Chinese have been cutting away at the population of the United States for years with fentanyl, social media, covid and via a variety of other methods. Now they have delivered the trojan horse to our front gates. We are in the process of opening the gate and welcoming it into our economic system. As Gordon Gecko said, greed is good. If the Bitcoin network and the crypto ecosystem in general continue to expand at the current rate, there will be billions and billions of dollars to be made by adopting the correct pro crypto strategy. The rich and powerful people of the US see dollar signs in front of them, so they are choosing to ignore the warning signs inside and outside of crypto. Warning signs like this:

Here is a headline from the July 29, 2023 news on msn.com: "A Chinese linked company was found running an unlicensed California biolab that contained at least 20 potentially infectious diseases, including coronavirus, HIV, hepatitis, and herpes. The illegal and unlicensed lab was full of lab mice, medical waste, and hazardous materials."

The lab had more than 900 genetically engineered mice in it. They also found thousands of vials of blood and suspected biological material.

If the Chinese are trying to destroy us with viruses, don't you think they might also be trying to destroy us via other methods as well?

CHAPTER 12 – CHINA AND RUSSIA

My neck is barking at me as I sit here in the middle seat, two hours into the 6 hour flight. Don't buy plane tickets at the last minute. That's the moral of the story. But the real issue is that I played basketball last night for the first time in months. The over-40 town league is starting up in a couple of weeks and I was secretly hoping that I might be able to play again this season. So I went last night to test things out before they hold the draft. I was freakin awesome. Blocks, steals, rebounds, gorgeous assists. Plus, I was 4-8 from downtown. And two of those 3's were from at least two feet behind the three point line. That qualifies as being on fire. I was the best player on the court by a mile.

But I can't play this season. My neck definitely wasn't feeling right after playing. Sleep was sporadic because I kept waking up needing to change my neck position. And today there is numbness going all the way down my arm into my left thumb and fingers. That's not a good sign lol. I just gotta admit that Im too old and beat up to play basketball anymore. The glory days are behind me. Last night was a good freakin way to go out though. Man I'm going to miss hoops. Getting old sucks.

I need to stop being such a pussy. We are headed to Vegas! Three and a half days of gambling and whatever else the city offers. A buddy is turning 50 and there is a group of us going out there to celebrate. I think there are 15 of us in total. We all love to gamble, but I'm definitely the biggest degenerate of the bunch.

The guys that put the trip together have reserved a cabana at the hotel pool for one of the afternoons. That's not really my scene, but I suppose it could be fun. They also have a reserved section at one of the strip clubs out there for one of the nights. Now THAT is my scene. 100%. I'm not planning to go with them that night though. That's a tough situation for marital partners to put the other in. Some relationships are cool with it. Some not.

My wife is not a jealous person by nature. Not at all. But this is not a typical situation. Some people might go so far as to say that I have an addiction to strip joints. During the course of my life, I would estimate that I have spent well over 100 grand in strip clubs. Been going for almost 30 years. Probably have gone an average of 20 times per year. Post divorce periods it was a heckuva lot more often than that. But even when I have been married I have gone "on the reg" as the younger generation might say. Average spent per night? I'd guess about 300 bucks. Heck I have been to Vegas more than 30 times and I have been to strip clubs on just about every one of those trips. Most nights out there I would spend at least 500. So 30 years, multiplied by 20 times a year, is 600. Multiply 600 by 300 (avg spent) and it comes out to $180,000. As I said, well over 100k spent in strip clubs during my lifetime.

Hot chicks are deserving of my cash. That's just how I look at it. But now that I am happily married, that is not a view that my wife necessarily agrees with. It makes her a little uncomfortable when I say "That lady is hot" or "Damn, look at her" or something along those lines.

"Would it be better if I thought these things and just didn't say them out loud?" I remember asking her one time. She answered "Yes". But I don't really think that is the case. She will know what I'm thinking. I'm a dude. It's just that simple.

Truth be told, my wife has a very strong point. I understand that me talking with scantily clad women who I find very attractive would make her uncomfortable, especially when she is in Russia with the kids. I never want to make her uncomfortable, so I'm not planning to go to the strip joint with the guys during this trip. Our conversation from last night is replaying in my mind right now. We have been talking on WhatsApp (video call) every night and I'm just glad she is cool with me going to Las Vegas.

"I'm not gonna go to the strip joint. There will be plenty of other things to keep me occupied out there."

"It's not like I don't want you to have fun," she says. "But this is a last minute thing and I didn't know anything about it until a few days ago. I just don't want you getting all drunk and paying all kinds of women to be rubbing all over you. I thought you said we needed to be careful with the money we are spending?"

She has a point.

"This is a one time thing. I probably won't be going back to Vegas again for years," I replied. "While you are gone I just want to be able to hang out with the guys. I don't need to go to the strip joint with them though. If that makes you feel not good, then I don't want to do it. I don't want you to feel jealous."

"It's not jealousy," she clarified. "It's just that I would rather be out there with you. I want to be there in Vegas having fun too."

"Well maybe we can try to go out there together sometime next year," I offered. "I'd love to go out there again with you. I'd rather go with you anytime. But I'm here alone for now, so it's just a good opportunity to hang out with a few friends that I haven't seen in years. I won't go crazy and I will watch how much money I spend gambling."

"Well if your friends are gonna go, I don't want you to have to miss out. Just make sure you be careful and stay in control." My wife is so cool.

"I'm not gonna go to the club. I have been to enough strip joints in my life. It's no big deal not to go," I said. I meant the words, but there was a part of me that was hoping she would more assertively tell me it was definitely ok.

"If you do, that's fine. It's up to you." Those were her last words on the matter. We said "I love you" to each other and said goodbye.

I love her so much. I really do. I'm not gonna go. I don't think.

Let's for a minute think back to when Vladimir Putin and Xi Jinping got together during the opening ceremonies of the 2022 Winter Olympics in Beijing, China. The meeting was a particularly big deal because there was no one from the Biden administration there at the Games. The US had announced that we weren't going to send any official diplomats to the Olympics in protest of what's going on with the Uighurs in China, a situation that truthfully I know almost nothing about. But to not send any high-level delegates to the Olympics was surely seen as a sign of extreme disrespect by China. The US and China are the two most powerful countries in the world. And if the US is going to outwardly disrespect China, it makes sense that China might then look to befriend the #3 most powerful country in the world: Russia.

The meeting between Putin and Xi was also a huge deal because there were 100,000 Russian troops positioned on the Ukraine border at the time. The world was on edge waiting to see what the next move from the Russians would be. As we all now know, the next move from Russia was to invade Ukraine, which they did a few days after the Winter Games were completed. China did not want the stain of this war to tarnish their Olympic Games while the eyes of the world were upon them, so Russia politely waited until the games were complete before initiating the invasion.

When Russia attacked Ukraine, they knew that sanctions from the international community would follow. These economic sanctions would hit directly at Russia's ability to exchange rubles for US dollars and euros on the world markets. As a result, Russia would likely need to increase their level of trade with other partners. China was more than willing to step in to fill the void. The fact that world trade operates largely on the US dollar and though the euro, well that's a weakness for both Russia and China. Both countries know it is a problem and it is one they would like to fix. What's the best way to do that? Teaming up seems like a good answer. The enemy of my enemy is my friend. Throughout history, Russia and China haven't been the closest of friends. They share a huge border with one another and there have been tensions that have arisen through time along that border. But this is a new day and age. It is time to rethink both economic and military alliances.

Russia and China obviously have a vested interest in partnering. Wrap in with that the benefits of an emerging decentralized financial system that can be used to circumvent sanctions and you have a holy grail win win type situation. The buildout of the crypto ecosystem and the expanded use of cryptos is a great thing for both Russia and China.

SIDE NOTE: IN JUNE OF 2023, RUSSIA'S LARGEST BANK, SVERBANK, ANNOUNCED THE INTRODUCTION OF CRYPTOCURRENCY TRADING SERVICES FOR THEIR CUSTOMERS.

CHAPTER 14: 11:11

JUST LIKE IN SOME HOTELS, WE ARE GOING TO SKIP A CHAPTER #13

I've been telling myself for years that if I ever do decide to write a book, I'm going to make sure to include what I have experienced during my lifetime regarding the number 1111. So here it is:

I was somewhere around the age of 25 when I realized that these numbers were not coming my way through some acts of sheer coincidence. It had happened enough times for me to know that there had to be a reason and there had to be a meaning. So I did what anyone else would do; I looked it up on the internet. I found that 11:11 indicates "angels are looking out for you". Well, there are actually a bunch of "definitions" associated with 11:11, but that's the one that holds the most relevance for me. **Angels are looking over me.** It just sounds comforting. I'm a religious individual, and through prayer I have fully accepted that whatever created us is still able to talk with us and hear us. The universe listens. That's my take anyway. And I'm not alone. There are plenty of people who agree with me.

For example - Paris Hilton has a company called 11:11 Media. She created the company in an effort to bring all of her business ventures together under one umbrella. Apparently 11:11 has always been her favorite time of day and she frequently tweets at that very time. "Make a Wish" is a popular message she likes to send in those tweets. I bring this up here for two reasons. One – Paris is an avid fan of crypto and NFTs. She is a strong influencer and it might be good for you to follow her on social media to hear about new projects she is getting involved with. Two – Paris is my Celebrity Hall Pass and if I ever get famous from writing this book I just want her to know that. So there it is.

During my twenties when I was gambling way more than I should have been, I would often just happen to look at the clock on a Sunday EXACTLY at 11:11. Sundays are NFL football days and at 11:11 on most Sundays back then I would be trying to figure out exactly which teams I would be betting and for how much. After seeing the 11:11 time jump out at me on a number of occasions, I started to notice an interesting trend: Anytime I saw 11:11, I always lost. Big. Like, every game I bet. Every. Single. Time. To the point where I eventually said "OK fine! I'm not going to bet when I see it!" It's just that simple, right? Im a glutton for *punishment but Im not a complete moron. Just don't bet when I see the numbers 1111. But then without fail every team that I was going to bet on would win. Something, somewhere was screwing with me.*

As time went on, I noticed the 11:11 affect in other areas of my life too. There would be days when I would see 11:11 and take notice of it, but then forget about it. Then later that day I would have a big fight with one of my soon to be ex-wives. Or I would get a speeding ticket. Or have an ultra bad day at work. It was like 11:11 became a huge neon light tipoff telling me to be careful. It happened so many times that it became ingrained into how I think. And it became important enough to me that I am now making space for it here in these pages. I encourage you all to stay alert for signs in life, whether they be 11:11 or some other form. Somebody or Something is out there and they talk to us every single day. It's just a matter of knowing how to listen.

Angels are looking after all of us…

When I see the numbers 11:11, I automatically say a quick prayer and thank you to God. The Creator. Whatever the heck it is that put us people here on earth. You can think what you want, but I believe that Charles Darwin was one of the most foolish human beings in history. To believe that human beings have gotten to this level of living here on earth - after starting out as mossy growths in water - is flat out insane. I'll say it. You people are out of your minds to 100% believe in evolution. Yes, of course, the earth and atmosphere has had an effect on how things grow and change through time. But my point is that THINGS HAD TO START SOMEWHERE! You can use all the fancy scientific talk that you want, but the world and the universe came from somewhere. Something created it. And if that "something" had the power to create this world, then it certainly has the power to help things evolve. To try to discount that reality away as a result of a "big bang" and Darwin's theory of evolution is simply ridiculous. It's just people feeling the need to explain something that can't be explained.

The power of someone who holds influence over others is immense. Our teachers tell us from a young age that humans evolved from amoeba and frogs and lizards and monkeys, etc. "You students don't need to think about this at all. We have done the thinking for you. Humans are all here as a result of evolution in nature."

I reject this thinking entirely. And I reject the premise that people don't need to think to come up with their own set of beliefs and explanations. Don't just blindly follow someone who wishes to influence your thinking!

Influencers in crypto are everywhere on social media. Hodl (It is awesome that spellcheck tries to automatically correct it to hold). Buy the dip. Have fun staying poor. These are the terms and phrases they use. They spread rumors and overexaggerate use cases and/or important updates to projects for their own benefit. For the most part, these people are only trying to get you and others to buy the coin because they are getting paid by the project to promote it or because they own a bunch of it and they want the price to go up! They are scammers. One simple "tweet" or post on Instagram can make them thousands or even millions of dollars! Please keep this in mind when making financial decisions.

There are a handful of influencers that I will briefly discuss now. These are among the most important people in the crypto industry.

ELON MUSK

When Elon tweets about crypto, people listen!

The man who shoots rockets to Mars and builds the best battery powered cars has been in the public eye with crypto users for years. During the bull run period in 2021, there were a handful of times when Musk would put up a "tweet" about Bitcoin or Dogecoin, and the market would immediately react. **INFO: Dogecoin is the first meme coin ever created. It was invented as a joke by a couple of software engineers back in 2013. They were poking fun at the wild speculation that was taking part in the cryptocurrency market at the time.** On Twitter, he legit would simply post a picture of the Dogecoin meme (a cute doggy looking thing), and the price of Doge would go up by 20% or more within minutes. Now that he actually owns Twitter (x)? Imagine the power.

Elon Mush has a ton of experience in the payments space. Earlier in his career he was a cofounder of Paypal and the suspicion amongst many is that he will someday find a way to integrate crypto as a payment feature within Twitter (x) as he builds out the ecosystem.

BITBOY

This is a controversial one. For a few years Bitboy, whose real name is Ben Armstrong, has run the largest crypto show on YouTube. He has positioned himself as a leader of the crypto community and a guy who wants to help people get more educated about crypto.

On the other hand, it has been proven that Bitboy is a scammer. I followed him for a period of time in 2021-22 and really liked the things that he had to say, so I added his thoughts into my decision-making knowledge base. One day, he suggested on his YouTube show that a coin called frontier (FRONT) was a good long-term investment because it was eventually going to be listed on Coinbase. That was a good enough pitch for me. **INFO: Coinbase is a US based crypto exchange that was founded in 2012. It has grown to become the largest US based exchange.** I bought FRONT at around three dollars a coin while his show was live on the air that day.

FRONT went up to about six dollars a coin within hours. Then it proceeded to go down and down. I sold somewhere around four dollars, but I continued to watch what happened. Within days that coin got smashed down to under 2 bucks, and now years later it sits at 19 cents per coin. There are plenty of people out there who didn't sell FRONT at a profit. Is it their fault that they bought the coin and held onto it and didn't sell? Yes of course it is. Personal responsibility is something I am a big believer in. But I hold contempt for Bitboy because he has scammed people time and time again. I've seen the circulating menu sheets that he hands out to prospective advertisers showing how much it costs for him to do a mention of a coin on his livestream. Seriously. He has a legit menu where it shows what the prices are for him to do certain activities to pump their projects. It is a scummy way to live and I just want to call it on the carpet right here.

MICHAEL SAYLOR

This is one of Bitcoin's biggest believers, and he has put his money where his mouth is. Michael Saylor, the longtime CEO of software vendor MicroStrategy, has led the company to adopt a financial strategy through which they use cash assets to acquire Bitcoin. And they keep on acquiring it. In late September of 2023, it was announced that MicroStrategy had acquired another 5,445 bitcoins for approximately $147 million in cash. This brings their total held as a company to more than 158,000 bitcoins.

The price of Bitcoin decreased immediately on the news. This seems like the opposite effect of what it should have, right? But Every. Single. Time. that MicroStrategy announces a new big purchase of Bitcoin, the market immediately tanks. It has become a social media trend at this point. I just wonder if it is really the retail public who is selling on these announcements? Or more likely it is just the whales who don't want to cede control to Saylor. If he amasses enough Bitcoin to move markets, he might become a worthy competitor in the game of price manipulation.

PlanB

F this guy. As far as I know, he is the only person who has ever blocked me on Twitter. And why did I get blocked? Because I called him a scammer. Which he is.

This guy was one of my most closely followed influencers when I first got into crypto. He had a beautiful chart called S2F (stock to flow) that showed the price cycle of Bitcoin against the halvening dates and the Bitcoin supply. Based on his chart, he was strongly projecting that the price of a Bitcoin was going to reach $100,000 during the bull run of 2021. That never happened. And as a result, I wasn't prepared for the downturn. Every move I was making back then was predicated on BTC going up to 100k. So when the price dropped from over 65k down to 55k in just a few days in November of 2021, I didn't react nervously. I just held tight. And I held tight all the way down to 16k. That was dumb. I have nobody to blame but myself. But I sure as hell ain't listening to this PlanB guy anymore.

CZ BINANCE

As I see it, the central character in all of crypto right now is CZ, the head of Binance. Binance is the largest crypto exchange in the world and they can make or break projects, coins, other exchanges, etc. The list goes on and on. Binance is the center of crypto and therefore CZ is the center of crypto.

When a coin gets listed on Binance, meaning that the coin will be available for trade on the Binance exchange, that causes a huge bump in the coin's price. So naturally, almost all small projects are looking to get listed there, and they pay fees to do so. It is a pay to play system, and CZ is the one who gets paid. Lots of power in a position like that...

Maybe too much power. In June of 2023, the Securities and Exchange Commission (SEC) of the United States announced that they were suing CZ Binance and the company. "Through thirteen charges, we allow that (CZ) and Binance entities engaged in an extensive web of deception, conflicts of interest, lack of disclosure, and calculated evasion of the law," said SEC Chair Gary Gensler.

THE WIZZ

Very few people reading this book will have any clue who this is. I don't know his real identity. I only know the Twitter account (@CryptoWizardd) and the incredible accuracy with which he predicts what is going to happen in the crypto market. The Twitter (x) account has over 500k followers as of September 2023. These followers have received the benefit of many pinpoint predictions regarding Bitcoin and a slew of other coins during the past few years. The account was telling people to buy LUNA when the coin was under two bucks apiece. You may remember that it went to over $150 at its' height........before it collapsed. Yes it came crashing down ultimately, but that's on you if you didn't sell a chunk prior to that.

I have watched The WIZZ Twitter account every single day for a couple of years. The degree of accuracy on his calls is uncanny. So accurate. Accurate to the point that I think this account must be a Chinese bot account used to signal their people for when BTC price rises and declines are about to happen. They then leverage trade off of the information. Sounds crazy, I admit. But the guy is that good. And I just wonder how in the hell he gets his info.

In case you are interested, a couple of his top calls for an expanded 2024 bull run post halvening are INJ (injective) and FET (Fetch.ai). Do with this info what you will. I own both.

SAM BANKMAN-FREID

Let's get to this piece of trash in the next chapter.

Chapter 15: THE FALL OF FTX

"Please God. Help me."

I have always believed in the power of prayer. It is kind of linked in with my belief in the power of the book The Secret. For those of you who haven't read it, you should. The central message of the book is that everything that happens to you in your life happens because you want it to. People usually have a difficult time believing this. But once you fully understand it, you realize that you can control the outcome of your life.

"God, Thank You for everything you have given me," I continued. "I have had such a great life. Yes there have been rough times, but the good times have always taken control eventually. The life I have been living with my family is everything I have ever dreamed of.

"I need some help right now. I'm not sure what to do. Can you please show me the way? I have made mistakes and I have taken my family for granted."

Plane rides back home from Vegas are always a grind. Exhausted. Anxious. Uncomfortable. I'm all of those things right now. Plus incredibly sad. I have to tell her. There's no way I can keep this to myself. She is still in Russia with the kids for a couple more weeks. I will wait until she gets back to tell her.

Some things happened while I was in Las Vegas that should not have happened. Everything just got out of control. I had too much to drink. Ate too many gummies. Smoked too much pot. I blacked out for a chunk of time, but I remember enough. I remember kissing that girl. I remember her putting her hand down my pants. The strippers in Las Vegas are just so damn aggressive. I was defenseless. Those tits right in my face. Her grinding on me. I remember all of this.

What I don't remember is how she ended up in the bed of my hotel room. I don't remember how I got there either.

"You still owe me $1,000."

Those words are stuck in my brain. I was still cranked when she said them, but something about the message snapped me back into consciousness.

Wow she is hot. "I thought I gave you about a thousand last night at the club?" I murmured.

"You did," she replied. "But you promised to give me another thousand when we got back to your room."

I watched her as she slipped on a pair of tight grey sweatpants. *What a physical specimen.*

"Can I send you venmo?" I asked, hoping the answer would be yes. The pockets of my pants from the night before were empty. I was cleaned out.

"Sure baby. That works."

She gave me her venmo. I sent her the payment. We hugged and she left. She had somewhere to be. And I needed her to leave.

What the fuck have I done?

"God. I am so sorry."

How much detail do I want to go into here? Everyone for the most part has already heard of Sam Bankman-Fried and the FTX downfall. If you haven't already heard about it, you probably live under a rock, and there is a next to zero chance that you would be reading this book, especially at this late stage in page numbers.

SBF fucked everyone. He thought he was smarter than everyone else. He made a move to grab the entire crypto industry by the balls. And he got punked. CZ Binance pantsed him in front of the entire world. And now SBF sits in a jail cell.

Let's talk about what happened with FTX. I am going to be as brief as possible here while giving as much detail as possible, and I will do this entirely from the top of my head, except for referencing the Internet for a couple of specific dates. Please excuse any "errors" that may appear through time - Some of these next bunch of paragraphs are based on my educated opinion of what happened, rather than being undisputed facts.

Sam Bankman Fried is a crypto mastermind. He started a company called FTX in 2019. FTX grew to become the third largest crypto exchange (by volume) in the world by July of 2021.

Prior to creating FTX, SBF co-founded a crypto trading and investment firm called Alameda Research in the year 2017. The quick growth of Alameda helped to pave the way for the creation of FTX in 2019, and the two entities worked very closely together. Too closely together, actually.

As Wikipedia says "According to public data reviewed by the Wall Street Journal, between early 2021 and March of 2022, Alameda Research amassed crypto tokens ahead of FTX announcing that they would list them." When FTX knew they would be listing a coin, they would tell Alameda and Alameda would go out and buy a bunch of the coin before FTX would make the listing announcement to the general public.

Through time, we have come to find out that it was actually his girlfriend, Caroline Ellison, who was the head of Alameda. The two lived together with other FTX employees in the Bahamas. **INFO: Caroline accepted a plea bargain for her role in the robbery of people's funds. She testified against SBF at his trial.**

As you can imagine, the link between Alameda and FTX was incredibly important from the jump. Yes, the coin listings shananigans was a piece of the cheating puzzle, but there were many other ways that the two companies worked together to screw people. The US government has accused Sam Bankman-Fried of wire fraud and conspiracy to commit money laundering, among other charges. These are just the charges the US thinks they can prove in a court of law.

The initial funding for FTX came from money made by Alameda. FTX then needed additional money thrown into the pot in order to grow the exchange as quickly as possible. THIS PART IS KEY. In late 2019, CZ Binance announced that Binance was making a strategic investment in FTX. This was certainly a great thing for the credibility of a new exchange like FTX was at the time. I don't know exactly how much Binance invested, but by 2021, the investment had paid off handsomely. Binance cashed out its holdings in FTX to the tune of $2.1 billion. This $2.1 billion was paid out in crypto – BUSD and FTT. **INFO: BUSD is a stable coin that is short for Binance US Dollar. BUSD is used in the Binance network to facilitate trading in and out of coins on the Binance exchange. FTT is the coin symbol for FTX coin, which was the proprietary investment coin within the FTX exchange. Holders of FTT coin would get benefits like cheaper fees if they held FTT in their FTX** exchange account. **As the FTX exchange grew, FTT coin grew in value along with it.** As part of the cashing out process, SBF gave FTT coin to Binance. A lot of it.

SIDE NOTE: THIS IS HOW SAM BANKMAN-FRIED GREW FTX SO QUICKLY: HE USED FTT COIN AS EQUITY FOR INVESTMENTS.

Here's how it worked:

Alameda would pay USD to FTX for FTT coins. Alameda would then use these FTT coins to invest in other crypto ventures. These businesses Alameda invested in could hold the FTT coins, or if they wanted to sell them, FTX would buy back the coins essentially by using the money that Alameda had originally given to them for those same FTT coins. Because FTX knew the timing and innerworkings of trades, as did Alameda Research, both of these companies could benefit from trades they knew would be coming onto the market. For example, let's say Alameda invests in company XYZ and gives them $10 million in FTT coin to finance the investment. Company XYZ says they will sell the FTT coin to get US dollars to finance their own projects. If FTX knew this large sell order of FTT would be coming onto the market, they would tell Alameda to sell FTT in advance. Alameda gets in first, sells a large chunk of FTT, and starts the price going lower. Then company XYZ's big sell trade of FTT hits the market, causing the price to drop more. Selling continues on down the line to the retail public. When FTX sees the sell orders start to dry up, they tell Alameda, who goes back in and buys up all the coins they sold..........at much lower prices than they originally sold them for. Ingenius! Alameda now has the same amount of FTT coins they started with and they have pocketed a bunch of profit in the process. These were the easiest bets of all time, based entirely on insider information.

As time went on, Alameda and FTX put too much FTT out into the market as collateral for their investments. The bear market started, and the price of FTT went down a bunch, as did the value of most coins. As the price of FTT was dropping, people at the companies who had accepted FTT as money for investment in their businesses got scared, so they started selling. Then so did retail. As this selling hit a pivot point, CZ Binance called in the big guns. In an incredibly unexpected development on 11/16/2022, he sold all of the remaining FTT that Binance had been holding since 2021 as part of the cashout of the initial investment in FTX. He announced it to the world via a tweet: "As part of Binance's exit from FTX equity last year, Binance received roughly $2.1 billion USD equivalent in cash (BUSD and FTT). Due to recent revelations that have come to light, we have decided to liquidate any remaining FTT on our books."

This tweet essentially initiated a run on the FTX exchange. The price of FTT coin crashed from $23 dollars on November 6, 2022 to under $3 dollars per coin three days later on November 9. As word spread about FTX being short of cash (and crypto), everyone started to sell whatever coins they held on the FTX exchange. Any and all coins. Days afterward, FTX admitted they were insolvent and halted all trading and withdrawals. SBF's FTX fortune had crumbled from $16 billion (estimated) to zero. And CZ Binance orchestrated the destruction! Why did he do this, you might ask?

During the 2020 United States election cycle, FTX was a huge donor to political candidates, especially on the democratic side of the aisle. In 2022, SBF stepped it up a notch further. Ahead of the November 2022 midterm elections, Sam Bankman Freid donated over $39 million to congressional democrats, a total bested only by left wing billionaire George Soros. **INFO: Soros is the devil.** While this political giving was going on, SBF was being praised in the US media as a Robin Hood type of figure who was looking to share his wealth with the poor throughout the world. But CZ Binance did not see SBF as a hero.

Throughout 2022, Sam Bankman Fried gained audience with Congress. He also met with Senior White House aids on at least 4 occasions in 2022 prior to the FTX collapse. During those discussions he attempted to cut out crypto exchanges that were based outside of the United States. He told political leaders that in order to correctly regulate crypto in the US, the government would need to allow only exchanges that are based in the US, so that their books could be verified for tax purposes, etc. This messaging hit home with legislators because crypto exchanges that are based in other countries do not need to follow the rules and laws of the US.

By delivering this message, SBF was attempting to elbow out Binance. And CZ wasn't having it. The Kingpin of Crypto initiated the FTT sell at just the right time to take down an enemy.

SBF fucked around. And he found out.

CHAPTER 16 – WHAT IF I'M RIGHT?

I knew I shouldn't have worn this shirt today. It's my favorite shirt. There's a big B on it and some Bitcoin looking artwork on the front. Nothing on the back. She only cared about the stuff on the front, anyways.

"I like your shirt. I'm into Bitcoin."

The words flowed effortlessly from her mouth as she smiled a big smile.

"Thanks," I replied. "It is so cool, isn't it? The whole crypto space gets me going." Did that come off in a propositioning type of manner? I think this to myself as I listen to her response.

"That's funny," she says, as her phone rings. She looks at the phone and pauses. "I have to take this call. I will let you know when the doctor is ready to see you."

I head to the corner of the room and take a seat near the window. That was a strange interaction. Or was it? Maybe I just think it was strange because she is good looking. That's just me thinking too much. Calm the fuck down.

The doctor visit was off to an interesting start. Sorry, I guess he is officially called a neurosurgeon. Don't want to undersell him as just a doctor. He has a much fancier professional title than that. And hopefully the title means he knows what the heck he is doing.

The neck doctor sure has a hot receptionist. I'll tell you that. It's just more fun when there is a good looking woman around. I'm sure she's not interested in me that way, but it's still fun just to feel the feeling. This feeling is wrong though. So wrong. It's the same type of feeling that got me fucking up in Vegas.

It has been two days since I've been back from Sin City. The first day back was horrible. My neck pain flared up like crazy that day. But worse was the guilt. I still can't get rid of the pit in my stomach. There's emptiness there. And it's my own fucking fault. And now I'm lying to her again on top of everything. We spoke yesterday on the phone and she asked about the trip to Vegas. Asked if I got any lap dances. I told her yes. Then she asked if anything happened that she should know about. I told her no. I'm a liar. But I just didn't know what I could possibly say. No words are going to help. She is in Russia with the kids and if I tell her the truth, I have no clue how she might react.

"Mr. (Anonymous), the doctor is ready for you now," the receptionist called out. "And so am I."

My head snapped up like a slingshot. Did she really just say that? I think to myself as I stand up from my seat. There's no way. I have to have imagined that. There was nobody else in the waiting room though, so there was nobody I could look at for a reaction to see if they heard the same thing. The time on the clock said 4:05. My appointment was scheduled for 3:45. We took X-rays at 3:45 and now I'm waiting to discuss the results of those X-rays with the neck doctor.

"I must be the last patient of the day, huh?" I asked as I approached the check in area. She rose to greet me.

"Yes. We saved the best for last," she replied playfully. "The bitcoin man. I would like to talk with you when you get out, if that's ok."

"Sure. That's cool. Let's hope I get some good news between now and then."

"Follow me," she said as she led the way down the hallway wearing a tight blue skirt and high heels. "First door on the right. You can have a seat in here. The doctor will be right in to see you."

And with that, she was gone. I'm sitting here in the neck doctor's office by myself, waiting to find out why my neck is on fire. Nonstop since I got back. Come to think of it, the only time during the past few days when I stopped thinking about this neck pain was two minutes ago when I was talking to the receptionist.

What the fuck? Why am I thinking about her? My wife and kids are who I need to be thinking about right now. How the hell am I going to tell her? She's going to be so crushed. Because of me. It's like life is fucking with me.

During our phone call last night, my wife asked me what I've been doing since I got back from Vegas. I told her I have been writing a lot. That, at least, was true.

"The book is almost done," I said to her at some point during the conversation.

"That's great!" she replied. "When will I get to read it?" She would be the first person to read the book once I got it finished. We had agreed on that previously. A couple of times. But that piece of info had slipped my mind.

"Good question," I responded. "It's not that close to being done yet actually, I guess. There is still a lot of editing I need to do. Gotta go through and correct all the spelling and grammar mistakes. It definitely won't be done before you get back."

I was drifting off in thought about our phone call as the doctor entered into the room.

"Mr. (Anonymous). It says here you are in some pain. I have your X-rays and I can see why." The doctor proceeds to tell me that I will need another surgery. The bracket-type thing that they put in my neck during the surgery from years ago had come loose in one area. This was causing friction against the nerves in that area of my neck. And that was causing the pain. I would need surgery to take the old bracket out. And then they would have to put a whole new one in. This one would be much better apparently, but the rehabilitation time would be at least three months. No picking up more than ten pounds during that time. I will have to wear a neck brace for at least the first month. Lots of time in bed for the first week after the surgery. Moving around will be difficult. I will need help.

"I can schedule the surgery for sometime next week," the doctor says as he looks at his computer.

"My wife is out of town until the end of next week. Maybe it would be better to schedule it for the beginning of the following week, if that's ok?"

"If you can deal with the pain until then, that is ok by me," he responded. "I can prescribe you something to try to help with the pain in the interim. How about the Monday of the following week?"

"That should work," I reply, as a feeling of helplessness flows over my body.

How am I going to tell her? How am I going to let her know that she is everything I have ever wanted in a woman. A partner. A beauty. A great mother. A friend. A lover. All of these things. And I have put them all in jeopardy.

I shake hands with the doctor as I head back out to the patient waiting area. There she is. That smile is so captivating.

"How did things go?" she asked.

"Could have been better. I'm going to need surgery." I watched as the smile on her face changed to a look of concern. *"It's ok. It happens. Gotta take the good with the bad and just stay positive."*

"That's a great way to look at things," she responds. We end up talking for a few minutes about crypto and what should be happening with prices as the halvening approaches. *"I am getting off work in just a couple of minutes. Would you like to go somewhere to continue talking?"*

What does she mean by somewhere? This is unbelievable. Why didn't shit like this ever happen to me when I was single? What a mindfuck. I'd like nothing better than to go somewhere and get drunk and forget about this pain for a few hours. But I can't.

"I'm sorry. I can't today. Maybe some other time?" We exchange numbers and make comments about being "crypto buddies". Then I say goodbye and leave the office. I don't think I can be crypto buddies with that woman. That's just not gonna help anything.

"I knew I shouldn't have worn this shirt today," I say quietly to myself as I head down the stairs.

Four words. What. If. I'm. Right?

That may technically be five words. But seriously. What if I'm right?

I mean, nobody ever thought that someone would hijack a plane and fly it into the World Trade Center. But someone did it. In fact, a bunch of someone's did and they flew planes into both World Trade Center buildings and the Pentagon and they tried to fly one into the White House too. A full-fledged, coordinated, well thought out, successful attack on the epicenter of our economy and our existence as a country. Why wouldn't you think it is possible for something like that to happen again?

I can't help but feel like it is September 10, 2001 and I'm trying to tell people that the policy of having plane hijackers go into the cockpit to speak with the pilot is an absolutely horrible, incredibly stupid idea. But nobody is listening. The airlines are making money and they see no reason to change anything. Don't worry, they tell me. I'm a conspiracy theorist, others say. OK, I respond, as I metaphorically shrug my shoulders. What else can I do? I'm just one man. And I need to worry about my own life.

Let's pause here for a moment and consider this: If I am correct, and China has meticulously grown Bitcoin step by step for the purpose of someday attacking the United States, when China does hit that sell button, what will happen? The answer will likely be determined based on a variety of factors....

Will the Bitcoin be sold solely on US exchanges or International Exchanges?
What is the price of BTC at the time of the selloff?
How low will the price go?
Will the US be in an actual military war with China at the time?
What is the status of the world economy at the time?
What other world events will come into play?

To envision the true impact of selling the Satoshi Bitcoin, we would have to be able to envision the state of the crypto infrastructure at the time that it all gets sold. Does it happen four years from now? Eight years from now? And how entrenched into the world economy is Bitcoin at the time of the selloff?

SIDE NOTE: THIS IS THE LAST SIDE NOTE OF THE BOOK. THANK YOU FOR READING.

Let's try to envision a scenario where the price of one Bitcoin is equal to one million US dollars in the year 2030. **INFO: Cathie Wood from Ark Investment Management predicts 1 BTC will be worth over $1 million by 2030.** Let's say that thousands of companies hold Bitcoin on their balance sheets at this time in the future, similarly to how MicroStrategy is doing now and how Tesla has done in the past. The crypto infrastructure throughout the world has grown by 2030, and Bitcoin is being used to settle transactions within seconds throughout the world. The big financial companies have built elaborate trading systems centered around Bitcoin. People are using a variety of different cryptos, but Bitcoin remains at the center of it all.

Things are moving along smoothly, and then one day Bam! Satoshi sells the entirety of his wallet. The price of one BTC immediately drops. How low? It is almost impossible to predict. But if roughly 5% of the entire supply of Bitcoin (1 million coins out of a 21 million coin supply) hits the market at once, a state of panic will ensue. The price drop will be a gut punch. And everyone in crypto will immediately understand that there is a coordinated attack going on.

Sell, sell, sell, sell, sell. It's all going under. Maybe the price of one BTC falls below 50k? That would be my guess. 50k seems like a high number today, but if it was at a million, 50k would seem like a horrific drop.

When this happens there will be a run on banks in the United States. The crushing drop in the price of Bitcoin will bleed over into equity markets and all investments worldwide. Everyone will want to get their money at the same time. Their worthless, debt ridden US dollars that aren't worth the paper they are printed on. Total chaos. This is what the future will look like.

The trojan horse of Bitcoin is at our gates.

CHAPTER 17 – NO WIN SITUATION

The past couple of days have been unbearable. I mean, picking them up at the airport was great. I swear the kids grew a couple of inches each while they were away. It was so nice to be able to hug them. Those hugs were healing. Kissing and hugging my wife was not healing though. It was tearing my heart out. And it has been tearing my heart out more and more every single time since she has been back. Two days of torture. And I still haven't told her.

"You aren't going to eat anything tonight?" she asks.

"Nope," I say back. "They told me I can't have anything except water. I need to have an empty stomach."

The surgery is tomorrow morning. The doctor says things should go smoothly and after a few months I should be on the road to being pain free. He said I shouldn't worry.

"Well then, I'm just going to heat up leftovers for the kids," she says. "What time do you need to be there in the morning?"

"8am," I reply. *It's gonna be a long night.*

I've never had to live with guilt like this before. Sure, I have messed up in the past. But never like this. And I sure as hell have never had to hide a lie like this before. It's killing me.

"He said the surgery should be done by about 12. I will need to spend one night there and should be ready to come home in the morning the day after." *If I still have a home to come home to...*

"Well I will plan to get there around noon then. Hopefully I will get to see you for a bit and then I will go get the kids from school. Then I will bring them back with me again to see you later in the afternoon."

"That sounds great," I reply. *It really does.*

As we lay down in bed and embrace later that night, I am more scared than I have ever been. I want to just tell her and get it over with, but I can't find the words.

Maybe she will find them for me.

"How's your book going?" she asks.

"Almost done," I tell her. "I'm right at the very end."

"Can I read it? Maybe I will have time tomorrow night while you are at the hospital."

I think to myself. She is going to read the book at some point. I promised her that she would be the first. Whenever she reads it, it's going to be horrible - for the both of us. Would it be better for her to read it AFTER I tell her what happened? She knows I've spent two years of my life writing this. Should I tell her I'm just throwing all of my writings away without anyone reading it? There's no way that's going to make any sense. I'm just gonna come clean and tell her right now.

"Yes. You can read it. I will give you a copy tomorrow in the morning before you drop me off."

And that's what I did.

On September 29, 2023, the Wizz (@cryptowizardd) posted on Twitter (x), "1 more #BTC run before real depression. Make sure to sell the top this time. Otherwise you are not going to make it over the next few years."

I can't help but wonder if this means that the Satoshi wallet selloff will be sooner than I expected. "1 more BTC run before the real depression". What does "the real depression" mean? Your guess is as good as mine.

The world seems to be inching closer and closer towards World War 3. Ukraine and Russia have been going at it for a couple of years, with the US and Europe heavily involved from the sidelines. Iran vs Israel is a teapot ready to boil. North Korea vs South Korea is always a spark away from igniting. And China is preparing every day for an invasion of Taiwan. Xi Jinping openly talks about it in speeches he delivers to his countrymen. They fly simulated air force attacks against Taiwan regularly. The US government has openly stated that they will defend Taiwan militarily if China does attack, although that public stance has changed at times, depending on who is talking. I'm actually not sure what the "official" stance is at this time. Will we defend Taiwan or not?

The point is - the world is in for a heap of trouble in the not too distant future. Wars and money. Money and wars. And power. These are the things that the governments and people in control are concerned about. They want to preserve and protect what they have accumulated.

Bitcoin is a threat to the status quo. But there is too much money involved for the large financial companies of the world to ignore it any longer. The Bitcoin spot ETF applications from Black Rock, Fidelity and others will be approved in the year 2024, if not before. There is a rather important US Presidential election coming up in November of 2024 and the party in power (democrats) will not want the lack of crypto clarity to cost them votes. There are many young voters in this country who own cryptocurrencies, and they want their crypto to go up in value. Gary Gensler, a democrat who heads the SEC, has put roadblock after roadblock in the way of legalizing and regulating crypto. And for that reason, the democrats are seen as the party holding crypto back. But if they can get legalization and regulation approved during the first half of 2024, they can take credit for the price increases that are sure to follow. This will help at the ballot box.

Some people might ask why I would recommend buying Bitcoin to people if it is eventually going to be used as a weapon against my country. That's a fair question. My answer would simply be that I believe, with the highest level of confidence possible, that Bitcoin will go up in value during the next few years. Way up. I want to take advantage of that for my own personal gain.

Besides, I'm just one person. One person who has never written a book before. Never published a book before. Bitcoin is going to do what Bitcoin is going to do, isn't it? Or am I supposed to expect that I can change the course of future history with the words contained in these pages?

The truth is that I have no clue what to do next. How exactly does someone go about getting a book published and available for people to read? I just did a google search asking this very question, and one of the results is that I can self-publish the book through Amazon. It seems kind of easy actually. So that's what I will probably do.

But how can I do it anonymously? I'd rather not have people know who I am. Satoshi didn't use his real name. And there is a reason for that. So I'm thinking maybe I shouldn't use my real name either. That's why the author is Anonymous.

But if anyone out there really wants to find out who I am, it won't be that hard. The way I see it, if this book gets to the point of popularity where people are actually putting in work to figure out who wrote it, then maybe that means I have written something good. Something that I can be proud of. And something that will educate people about a topic that they need to learn about. Our very existence weighs in the balance.

Signed, Anonymous

Made in the USA
Columbia, SC
08 December 2023

e5810240-17d9-4fa9-9068-e4b4c995e6dcR01